HEAVEN-SENT
MIRACLES
& RESCUES

ANDREA JO RODGERS

HARVEST HOUSE PUBLISHERS
EUGENE, OREGON

Published in association with The Steve Laube Agency, LLC, 24 W. Camelback Rd. A635, Phoenix, Arizona 85013.

Cover design by Bryce Williamson

Cover Photo © Chalabala, imagedepotpro / Getty Images

Interior design by Aesthetic Soup

For bulk, special sales, or ministry purchases, please call 1-800-547-8979.
Email: Customerservice@hhpbooks.com

Heaven-Sent Miracles and Rescues
Copyright © 2022 by Andrea Jo Rodgers
Published by Harvest House Publishers
Eugene, Oregon 97408
www.harvesthousepublishers.com

ISBN 978-0-7369-8528-4 (pbk.)
ISBN 978-0-7369-8529-1 (eBook)

Library of Congress Control Number: 2022931412

Printed in the United States of America

22 23 24 25 26 27 28 29 30 / BP / 10 9 8 7 6 5 4 3 2 1

This book is dedicated in loving memory of my
dear friend Elizabeth "Betty" Heilos—a compassionate
and highly skilled nurse who helped so many with her
medical knowledge combined with the power of prayer.

. . . .

Also, a special thank you to the Joan Dancy & PALS
(People with ALS) Foundation for helping patients
and families battling amyotrophic lateral sclerosis
(also known as Lou Gehrig's disease). You can
learn more about this wonderful charitable
organization at www.joandancyandpals.org.

Acknowledgments

A special thank you to my proofreaders: Rick, Thea, and Katy. Thank you to my literary agent from The Steve Laube Agency, Bob Hostetler, for his support. Also, a giant thank-you to editors Kim Moore, Amber Holcomb, and Kathleen Kerr at Harvest House Publishers for their professional guidance.

Contents

1. Into the Darkness 9
2. Rising Waters 17
3. Fire and Ice 23
4. Surrounded by Love 31
5. Rock Bottom 39
6. Anything for Ice Cream 47
7. Clamp It 61
8. The Tuck In 67
9. Saying Goodbye 77
10. Wading Through a Winter Wonderland 89
11. Dance Till You Drop 97
12. Puddle Jumping 107
13. By the Cross 115
14. Going to the Dogs 125
15. The Unexpected 133
16. The Journey 139
17. Preserving Memories 147
18. Keeping the Faith 153
19. The Nosebleed 161
20. Survival 171
21. Eyes Wide Open 183
22. Too Much Turkey? 189
23. Beating the Odds 195
24. Orchestrating a Miracle 205

Volunteer Members of the Pine Cove First Aid and Emergency Squad

Jessie Barnes—optometrist

Colin Branigan—actor with the local theater group

Kerry Branson—architect

Mason Chapman—auto mechanic

Jillian DeMarco—library volunteer

Joshua DeMartin—community-college student

Cody Downs—veterinary technician

Genevieve Fitzsimmons—florist

Colleen Harper— speech-language pathologist

Archie Harris—retired state employee

Scott Jurgenson—high school junior interested in the medical field

Sadie Martinez—dental hygienist

Helen McGuire—nurse

Chris Nicholson—computer analyst; also, a volunteer firefighter

Ted O'Malley—retired from a career in the national park system

Meg Potter—social worker

Andrea Jo Rodgers (the author)—physical therapist and a 30-plus-year volunteer reflecting on first aid calls from her years on the rescue squad

Jose Sanchez—retired from a career in politics

Buddy Stone—retired pharmaceutical salesman

Greg Turner—retired electrical engineer

Alec Waters—seasonal special officer for the police department and a college student planning to become a veterinarian

Darren Williams—retired from a long career with the armed forces

Members of the Pine Cove Police Department

Officer Ethan Bonilla

Officer Jack Endicott

Sergeant Derrick Flint

Dispatcher Jerome Franklin

Officer Kyle Jamieson

Officer Vinnie McGovern

Officer Evan Pearce

Officer Brad Sims

Officer Don Woods

Paramedics

Rose Anderson

Frederick Dixon

Ty Fleming

William Moore

Brenda Nielsen

Paula Pritchard

Kennisha Smythe

Arthur Williamson

1

Into the Darkness

You, LORD, are my lamp;
the LORD turns my darkness into light.

2 SAMUEL 22:29

The rain, which began as a light drizzle yesterday, fell hard and steady. Intermittent breezes transitioned to strong, sustained winds. A powerful nor'easter bellowed its arrival at the shore town of Pine Cove.

DISPATCHER: "Request for the fire department and first aid squad at 118 Bergen Street for a general fire alarm."

"Here we go again," Jessie Barnes said as our first aid pagers blared an alert. When Jessie wasn't working as an optometrist, he spent time volunteering as an emergency medical technician (EMT) with the Pine Cove First Aid Squad. Today, that meant standing by at the squad building and making sure emergency services were available to town residents during the storm.

The relentless winds had led to a steady stream of fire alarms all afternoon. We'd taken turns answering the calls. Now, several squad members went downstairs to the bay area in case an ambulance was needed at 118 Bergen Street. The rest of us set up air mattresses in the front room of our first aid building.

Pine Cove is a small town, so normally we respond to first aid calls from our homes. When our pagers go off, we drop whatever we're doing to answer the call. Today, with the hurricane-force winds and the looming threat of tidal flooding, we decided to stay at the squad building. We knew it would be much too dangerous to attempt driving to headquarters during the height of the storm. I felt guilty leaving my family but realized we'd need as many hands as possible on deck.

Jose Sanchez breezed into the squad's meeting room. After retiring from a long government career, Jose began volunteering as an EMT because he wanted to serve the community. "They didn't need us on the Bergen Street fire alarm. I've also got some good news. So far, there's no flooding anywhere in town, not even along Ocean Boulevard."

Pine Cove is surrounded by water on three sides. There's the Atlantic Ocean to the east, Jensen's Pond at the southern end of town, and Pebble Lake at the northern border. A few times over the years, the southern end of town near Jensen's Pond has flooded with several feet of water. Mostly, it has caused damage to people's basements. Expensive to repair, but nothing life-threatening.

"I can't believe just four days ago, weather forecasters were still uncertain about the path of the storm," I said. Some weather models had predicted it could directly strike the shore, while others indicated it would turn out to sea. Now, it appeared a direct hit was imminent.

Jessie glanced at his wristwatch. "Well, time will tell. High tide is at eight o'clock. Two hours to go."

Just then, the lights flickered. A few seconds later, our generator began humming. I glanced out the front windows and noticed the entire street had been plunged into darkness.

Greg Turner's cell phone buzzed. He checked the screen, then told us, "I just heard the entire town is without power." Greg had recently retired from his job as an electrical engineer. Analytical yet compassionate, he contributed much to our squad.

DISPATCHER: "Request for first aid at 302 Cherry Blossom Lane for a fall victim with a leg injury."

Jessie clipped his portable radio onto his waistband. "Greg, Andrea, and I will handle this. The rest of you can hold down the fort here."

I shoved my cell phone into my pocket and pulled on my raincoat as we rushed downstairs to our "first run" ambulance. Our squad owns three rigs. Each month, we alternate which will be the first to respond to calls. That way, they get even use.

I climbed into the back and gathered some of our equipment, including a clipboard, gloves, and a flashlight.

"We're responding to Cherry Blossom," Jessie told dispatch as he drove the ambulance out of the building. In the darkness I heard, rather than saw, the rain pounding on the roof of the rig. The fierce winds rocked the ambulance. Instinctively, I tightened my seat belt.

I initially joined the first aid squad more than 30 years ago when I was entering my senior year of high school. One day, while I was working in the beach office selling badges, Special Officer Alec Waters told me he was a volunteer with the Pine Cove First Aid and Emergency Squad. He said he oversaw the cadets (members under the age of 18) and asked me to join. At first, I said no. I was busy with school, track, and my summer job. But for every reason I gave not to join, he countered with one that I should. Eventually, he convinced me. Since then, I've answered more than 9,000 first aid and fire calls.

When we arrived in response to the call that dark night, Jessie maneuvered our ambulance behind a police car. "The house is on the right."

As I stepped out the side door, the wind nearly ripped the handle from my hand. I used my body weight to close the door. While Greg pulled the trauma bag out of a side compartment, Jessie turned on the side floodlights to better illuminate the scene.

The house, a light-colored Colonial, stood a hundred yards back from the road. A large oak tree, a victim of the wind, had fallen across the driveway and part of the front lawn. The ambulance's flashing lights cast strange shadows as the leaves and branches waved violently. The three of us trekked slowly across the yard, taking care to skirt around the branches of the downed tree.

"Watch those wires!" Greg shouted over the wind and rain.

I noted the large black cables that snaked across the yard. *Thank goodness the power is off.* If it suddenly returned and the wires became live, I feared we could be electrocuted. As we drew farther away from the ambulance's floodlights, my flashlight's beam lit the way through the pitch-blackness.

Officer Jack Endicott met us at the front door. "Your patient's name is Tip Custer. He's got a nasty cut on his leg. Follow me." As an officer, Jack Endicott was following in the footsteps of his father and grandfather, who had been "men in blue" before him. Reliable and dedicated, he's an invaluable asset to the Pine Cove Police Department.

"Lead the way," Jessie replied. We followed Officer Endicott across a small foyer and up a carpeted staircase. I held on tightly to the handrail with my free hand to avoid tripping in the darkness.

A woman stood in the hallway. She held a long, white tapered candle, which cast a warm glow across her face. She pointed toward one of the bedrooms. "Thank you so much for coming. My husband's in there."

Tip, a middle-aged gentleman with a bushy beard, sat on the edge of a queen-size bed, with his left foot on the floor and his right resting on the mattress. "I'm so sorry to bring you out in this," he apologized. "We don't normally live here. This house belongs to friends of ours. They're letting my wife and me stay here because of the storm. When the lights went out, I didn't have a flashlight with me. I accidentally tripped over the rug and fell into that glass table."

After we introduced ourselves, Greg peeled back the bath towel that Tip had wrapped around his lower leg. Officer Endicott and I shined our flashlights onto the wound so that we could get a better look. A long, deep, jagged cut ran along the outside of Tip's calf. Shards of glass littered the floor.

"I'm afraid you're going to need stitches," Jessie said. "We'll take you to the hospital. They can clean out the glass and sew you up."

Tip grimaced. "I kind of figured you were going to say that."

Mrs. Custer shuddered. "Thank goodness you can take him. I couldn't imagine trying to drive in this storm."

Greg began pulling out bandages, conforming stretch gauze rolls, and a sterile water bottle from our trauma kit. We'd need to gently cleanse the wound before bandaging it.

"I'll go back down and get the stair chair," I offered. Given the extent of Tip's injury, I knew he wouldn't be able to climb downstairs. The stair chair is designed to move patients safely down a flight of stairs using collapsible treads.

As I headed out the front door, I aimed my flashlight's beam into the darkness in front of me. Torrential rain hammered the ground, and I held on to my hood with one hand so that the winds wouldn't yank it off my head. Once again, I carefully stepped over the wires in the yard. I wasn't sure if they were cable, telephone, or electrical wires, but I wasn't taking any chances.

As I got closer to the ambulance, the floodlights lit up numerous large tree branches that swayed ominously in the wind. I had read stories about people getting killed by falling trees. Personally, I didn't care to become a statistic. *Anyone with even a shred of common sense is safely indoors.* The only people outside right then were either first responders or plain nuts. Or maybe both. I could picture the headline: *Volunteer EMT Crushed by Large Tree.* I shivered and pushed the thought aside. At that moment, I placed my trust in God to keep me safe.

I trudged back to the house carrying the heavy stair chair. The wind caught hold of it, and I struggled to keep it tucked under my arm. Once I got safely inside, I tried my best to dry it off.

"It was bleeding pretty good when it first happened. At least it's not bleeding through the bandage yet," Tip said as I entered the bedroom.

I set up the stair chair and placed it next to Tip. "If it does, we can always add another layer."

Jessie patted the seat of the stair chair. "We're going to help you pivot to the chair. Put your weight on your good leg," he instructed.

Officer Endicott and Greg set up our stretcher on the front porch. After carrying Tip downstairs, Jessie and I maneuvered him from the stair chair to the stretcher. We covered him with a blanket and anchored it with seat belts. I placed a towel over his head and tucked in the ends under the edges of the blanket.

Mrs. Custer gave Tip a peck on the cheek. "I'll come get you when the storm subsides enough that it's safe to drive."

Tip squeezed his wife's hand. "Okay, thanks. I love you, honey. I'm sorry to have to leave you alone like this."

We rolled the stretcher off the porch and into the raging storm. As we hauled it across the wet grass and through large mud puddles, each of us held on to a corner of the cot to keep it steady. We loaded (a very wet) Tip into the back of the ambulance.

Jessie picked up the radio mic. "We're going to be transporting one from this location to Bakersville Hospital."

"Be advised, Highway 13 is flooded and not passable at this time," Dispatcher Jerome Franklin replied. Dispatcher Franklin, a veteran member of the Pine Cove Police Department, was well liked and respected by the officers for his intelligence and efficiency.

Highway 13 is the route we normally take to the hospital. Unfortunately, now that wasn't an option. We'd have to take Route 4 instead. While Highway 13 is a two-lane highway with stores on each side of the roadway, Route 4 is a four-lane highway without any commercial or residential properties. I'd have much preferred to be able to stay on a highway that was surrounded by houses and buildings. Route 4 would be downright desolate. If we crashed or got stuck, there would be no help within easy walking distance.

"Received. Highway 13 is closed. We're going to take Route 4 instead. Let me know if you hear of any other closures." Jessie turned the windshield wipers to the maximal speed, but they weren't moving nearly fast enough to keep up with the tremendous downpour.

"If you're okay on your own back here," Greg told me, "I'll go up front with Jessie to act as another set of eyes. He could probably use a copilot."

I nodded in agreement. "Good idea. We'll be fine." I took the wet towel off the top of Tip's head and replaced it with a dry one, then cinched up my seat belt.

Only a minute or two passed before I heard Greg say, "Hang on. We've got a tree blocking the road. We're going to have to go over the curb to get around it."

Jessie maneuvered the ambulance over the curb onto Route 4's grassy edge. I gripped the bench seat until we came back onto the pavement.

Tip frowned. "We're off to a rough start. Do you think we'll make it there?"

Honestly, I wasn't sure. What if more trees blocked our path? However, I did my best to sound reassuring. "Yes, Jessie's a great driver."

We crawled along, working our way closer to the hospital. Rain pelted the roof of the ambulance, creating a dull roaring noise. Gale-force winds lashed the vehicle, causing it to shake.

Normally, it takes 12 minutes to get to the hospital. After about 30 nail-biting minutes, Jessie pulled into the hospital's emergency department (ED) unloading area.

When we entered the ED, I heard the buzzing of generators. Patients on stretchers lined the hallways. We rolled past an elderly woman in a floral nightgown who was clutching her oxygen mask, as well an older man rubbing his stomach and gripping a yellow emesis (vomit) basin.

After veteran triage nurse Maggie Summers finished assessing a maternity patient, she listened to our report. "You can put Tip on that stretcher over there," she said, pointing to the far wall.

Jessie, Greg, and I lifted him from our stretcher to the hospital's. "At least you're on a dry sheet now," I said.

"I can't thank you enough. I can't believe you had to go to so much trouble for me," Tip said.

Greg shook Tip's hand. "That's what we're here for. They'll give you some stitches, and you'll be as good as new."

As we rolled our now-empty stretcher out of the hospital, more patients came rolling in. Even as the storm raged, the ED was filling up.

"With trees coming down, I'm concerned Route 4 may have become impassable by now. Let's stick with local roads and try Throckmorton Street instead," Jessie suggested.

"I'll drive back and give you a break," Greg offered, so Jessie switched to the passenger seat. After tidying up the rear of the ambulance, I buckled myself into the captain's chair, which is directly behind the front cab. When we started moving, I pivoted in my seat so that I could look out the front windshield.

Intersections normally controlled with traffic lights were now completely dark. Greg stopped at each one before proceeding. Fortunately, there were no other vehicles on the road except for an occasional emergency vehicle.

Howling winds screamed like lonely feral cats looking for company. As I watched the heavy rains pounding against the windshield, I didn't envy Greg the task of driving us back to the squad building.

We left the local highway and turned right onto Throckmorton Street. Normally, I admire the quaint shops that line the street. Tonight, I couldn't even see them.

Our rig threaded through the inky blackness, heading ever so slowly toward a small drawbridge. The bridge, which spans an inlet that leads to the Atlantic Ocean, provides passage from one town to the next.

I admit I can be a backseat driver. I'm the kind of person who taps imaginary brakes if I think the driver doesn't have a safe following distance. Sometimes, I offer my (unwanted) opinion.

About three blocks from the bridge, I suddenly tensed. My eyes strained to see what lay in the darkness in front of us. I yelled, "Stop the rig!"

Greg hit the brakes. "What's the matter?"

"I think I see water up ahead," I said. For a second, I thought I was gazing at an enormous puddle. Then, realization dawned. The inlet had flooded its banks.

We stared ahead in shocked disbelief. If the floodwaters had reached this far before high tide, it was an ominous sign indeed.

"Now Route 4 is the only way home," Jessie said. "There will be even more trees down. Let's hope we can make it."

Greg made a U-turn, reversing our course and pointing us back in the direction of Route 4. It took well over a nail-biting hour before we finally backed safely into our ambulance bay. By the grace of God, we made it safely home. At the time, we didn't know the worst was yet ahead.

2

Rising Waters

Let all the faithful pray to you
while you may be found;
surely the rising of the mighty waters
will not reach them.

PSALM 32:6

After I peeled off my raincoat, pulled off my boots, and washed my hands, my stomach grumbled loudly. The smell of pizza wafted tantalizingly through the air.

"Fortunately, the pizzeria has a generator. They dropped off some pies for us. Help yourself," Jose Sanchez said.

"That's terrific." I began wolfing down a slice, worried we'd have another first aid call before I could finish it.

Jose passed me a bottle of water. "I've been watching the weather report. The storm is intensifying. High tide will be here soon."

Residents who live close to the ocean and our town's lakes and ponds were asked to evacuate in advance of the storm. As far as I could recall, we had never done that before. Somehow, this storm was different. Bigger. Scarier. "I wonder how high the storm surge will be."

"No one knows for sure. Fingers crossed," Jose replied.

I took a swig of water. "I'm glad everyone's been evacuated, just in case it gets hairy by the water."

Jessie looked up from his crossword puzzle. "It's almost high tide now. The emergency management team just reported so far, so good. There's still no significant flooding anywhere in town."

"I wonder if it's possible for us to escape without serious flooding?" Helen McGuire asked. As soon as Helen had finished her nursing shift, she'd come straight to the first aid building to stand by in case we had calls. Her husband, Skeeter, a volunteer firefighter, was standing by at the firehouse.

"Let's hope so," Greg replied. No sooner had he uttered the words than our first aid pagers began beeping.

DISPATCHER: "Request for the fire department and first aid squad at 201 Jefferson Avenue for a water rescue assignment."

I crammed the last bite of pizza into my mouth and pulled my rain boots back on.

"I'll take Greg, Jose, Genevieve, and Cody. We'll bring two rigs," Jessie said. Genevieve Fitzsimmons and Cody Downs joined our rescue squad about 12 years ago. They're both solid contributors to our department.

When I realized I wasn't going on this call, I paused to swallow my pizza. Just then, Cody's phone rang. He glanced at the screen and then turned to me. "I have to take this. Could you please go for me?" he asked.

"Of course," I replied. I was eager to see how much the water levels had risen since our last first aid call. Although I was a certified lifeguard when I was younger and have taken water and ice rescue courses, I've only been on one other water rescue call related to flooding during my years on the squad. During that previous storm (much tamer in comparison to this one), we had stayed with our ambulance, and the firefighters had brought the people who needed to be evacuated over to us. I assumed this call would be the same.

When I climbed into the back of the ambulance, Jessie tossed me a Gumby suit. "Just in case," he said. A Gumby suit is a waterproof suit that guards against hypothermia if the wearer is immersed in cold water. Ours are fluorescent yellow. They have built-in boots and gloves, as well as a hood. I had only worn it during drills in Pine Cove Lake. Never on an actual rescue call.

I took off my boots and thrust my feet into the suit. Once I pulled it up and put in my arms, Greg helped me secure the hood. Even as I donned the suit, I didn't really think I'd be entering the water. I pictured myself standing at the water's edge, ready to help if necessary.

"You ready yet? Let's go," Jessie said when we arrived on the scene. He led me to where members of the fire department stood near an aluminum boat perched close to the water. I trailed after him, trying to get my bearings. It looked as though we were parked on a residential street, about half a block away from Pebble Lake. The Atlantic Ocean's surging waters had merged with the lake, causing floodwaters to cascade into the neighborhood.

Even though we were two blocks from the beach, I could hear the pounding surf. The ferocious winds bowed the tops of the tall trees that lined Jefferson Avenue. Wind-driven rain fell in sheets, bouncing off the pavement. In the distance, I saw a dim light. Since the power was still out, I wondered where the light was coming from.

Jose handed me a flashlight. "Be careful. The people are in the last house on the right side of the street."

"Thanks." I cast the beam into the darkness. One firefighter was already wading through the water toward the house. Two others gripped the left side of the boat, and Jessie held the front right corner. At first, it was so dark I didn't recognize the firefighters. Then I realized they were Captain Jarrod Sanders and veteran member Bernie Quinn, two of our finest. I knew they'd have a solid plan for rescuing our victims.

"Grab on. Chuck Walling went ahead to see what we've got," Jessie said.

I grabbed the rear right corner of the boat, and we began pushing it into the water. A large orange basket stretcher had already been placed in the boat. Since it was made of a floatable material, we'd be able to use it during the rescue.

"We need to make sure we stay off the road. The manhole covers may have been displaced by the force of the water," Jarrod said. I shuddered at the sheer power of the storm surge.

The water gradually grew deeper until it reached my knees. "Watch out for that pine tree. It looks like it's coming down!" a fireman behind us shouted. I looked overhead to see the branches of a pine waving wildly in the wind, the trunk bending dangerously.

We pushed the boat across a neighboring yard and through a tall privet hedge. Once we cleared the hedge, I discovered the source of the light I'd seen earlier. A small red car stood in the driveway, submerged up to its hood. The water must have short-circuited its electrical system, causing the headlights and interior lights to come on.

As we pushed closer to the house, the water became deeper, until it was waist high. The rear of the ranch house was lit by the glow of the car's lights. Small waves lapped against the home's stone walls. Those walls provided us with a small amount of protection from the wind.

Chuck, the firefighter who had gone ahead of us, stepped out the back door of the home. "I'm going to bring out the husband first." He ducked back inside.

As I peeked through a large window, I saw the dim outline of furniture floating throughout the home. My eyes opened wider. I could see an elderly woman *floating on her bed.*

Chuck returned with an older man in his arms. Together with Jarrod and Bernie, they hoisted him first onto the roof of the car and then eased him down into our boat.

"I'm going to stay back with Chuck," Jarrod said. "We'll get Mrs. Burton secured into the basket stretcher while you take Mr. Burton out in the boat."

I held the front left side of the boat with both hands, managing to keep the flashlight balanced between the edge of the boat and my right hand. I pointed the beam straight ahead into the blackness.

Mr. Burton gripped the sides of the boat tightly. "Thank you. My wife can't walk. I don't know what we'd have done if you hadn't come."

"We're going to go back and get her next," Jessie promised.

We lapsed into silence as Bernie, Jessie, and I focused on navigating through the current. We gradually made our way back toward the fire trucks and ambulances. This time, instead of going through the hedge, we hugged the sidewalk, making sure to stay off the road.

As we drew closer, the emergency lighting from the fire trucks lit the area. When we entered shallow water, many strong arms lifted Mr. Burton from the boat to safety.

"Time to turn around and do it again," Jessie said. We began our trek back toward the house. Although it was cold outside, I was sweating from exertion.

As we approached the ranch house for the second time, the water grew deeper and deeper. Now it was up to my chest. Thank goodness we'd arrived when we did. With the water still rising, there was nowhere higher for the Burtons to seek refuge. I shuddered to think of what could have happened.

Jarrod met us by the back door. "Andrea, you stay here and hold the boat against the wall. Chuck and I already secured Mrs. Burton in the basket stretcher. I want the rest of you to help us carry her out."

The men stepped inside, and I suddenly found myself alone. I was glad the car was still casting a glow across the driveway, erasing a small degree of the blackness. I was determined not to let the boat get swept away by the wind and waves.

I braced myself and held the boat against the home with my full body weight. I cast my flashlight beam through the window into the home and could just barely make out the figures of the rescuers as they helped Mrs. Burton.

I tried to block out the fact that I was scared. I don't have a great track record with water and darkness. Years back, my son and I were in a terrifying elevator accident in which our elevator car crashed into the building's basement and quickly began filling with water. It was through the grace of God we survived.

I refocused my thoughts on the present. The water level continued rising, and I felt waves splashing near my shoulders. I tightened my grip on the boat. If I could have seen my knuckles through the thick rubber gloves of the Gumby suit, I knew they'd be turning white. In that moment of solitude, I prayed, *Dear God, please keep us safe.*

The back door was suddenly thrust open, and Jarrod, Bernie, Chuck, and Jessie stepped into the raging storm. They waded through the rising water and lifted Mrs. Burton, safely secured within the basket stretcher, into the boat. She looked frail, and I could read the worry in her eyes. My heart went out to her. A ruthless nor'easter had destroyed a lifetime of photos and personal treasures. Maybe even the structure and integrity of her very home. But at least, for now, she and her husband were safe.

Once again, I stood at the front left corner of the boat. I gripped Mrs. Burton's lower leg with my right hand to prevent her and the basket stretcher from sliding. I cradled the flashlight in my other hand while I braced it against the edge of the boat. I took one last glance back at the flooded house.

Since the water was higher now, it was tougher going. I was glad we had the extra sets of hands to help push the boat. As we got closer to the fire trucks, I heard one of the firemen shout out, "Look out for that tree!"

It was the same pine tree that had looked like it was going to crash down when we first arrived. If it fell now, it would land directly on us. All we could do was push onward, hoping it wouldn't come down at that moment. Since we were in deep water, it wasn't as if we could "make a run for it."

The water became shallower as we approached the emergency vehicles, and it became easier to walk. A team of firefighters met us at the boat and lifted Mrs. Burton onto our ambulance stretcher. They wheeled her out of the windswept rain and into our warm, dry rig. Now, it was time for our EMS crew to begin our long, difficult trek to the hospital.

The storm raged on that night. Immediately following the call for the Burtons, we responded to a second water rescue call. During the wee hours of the morning, our first aid and fire departments responded to an additional 25 alarms.

Nowadays, we have a special water rescue team to respond in case of floods or other water-related emergencies. But I'll never forget being part of the rescue that night—and how God protected us.

Fire and Ice

When you walk through the fire,
you will not be burned;
the flames will not set you ablaze.

ISAIAH 43:2

A sher Lee pushed his walker out of the way, settled back in his recliner, and put up his legs. He glanced out the frost-lined window of his upstairs den and suppressed a shiver. Darkness had fallen on one of the coldest nights of the year. He tossed a flannel blanket across his lap and picked up a magazine from the small table next to him.

Content to be relaxing in warmth, he perused an article about polar bears in their natural habitat. Engrossed in the plight of the animals, he lost track of time. About an hour later, a loud bang from the next room jarred him from his reading. His heart rate quickened.

He struggled to his feet. He'd been meaning to get one of those electric recliners that help raise you up to make it easier to stand. Severe arthritis in his hips and knees from years of playing football were taking a toll on him. Nowadays, it was a major struggle just to get up and down a flight of stairs.

Using his rolling walker to support himself, Asher slowly made his way to his bedroom and pushed open the door. His eyes widened in surprise. Thick smoke billowed from his television. A small orange flame crackled at the base of the TV.

Asher hesitated. What should he do? Should he try to beat back the flames on his own? If yes, what could he use? The nearest fire extinguisher was downstairs in the kitchen.

No, he'd never be able to get the fire out on his own. He needed help. He eyed the telephone across the room on his night table. *I need to call 911.*

Even as he dialed, the flames grew larger. "Your call cannot be completed as dialed." Asher pushed the disconnect button and tried to dial again. Once more, the call failed. Fear crept into the pit of his stomach. *What should I do?*

Heavy smoke filled the room. Bright orange flames shot to the ceiling. Time was running out. Asher knew his best chance now was to try to get outdoors, but he feared he wouldn't be able to make it down the stairs fast enough to escape the flames. Desperately, he dialed 911 again. Once more, the call didn't go through. *Did the fire damage my phone line?*

Coughing from the heavy smoke, Asher pushed his walker toward the doorway. *Why is the fire spreading so quickly?*

. . . .

Dora Winn shivered despite having the heat cranked up in her car. Thanks to a last-minute assignment from her new boss, she'd gotten out of work 30 minutes late. After a long, nail-biting commute home on icy roads, she was relieved to finally pull onto Ridge Road. She knew her mother had kept her favorite dinner—Swedish meatballs—warm for her.

Dora's car slid on a patch of ice, and she downshifted to regain control. Just a few houses away from where she lived, a bright flash caught her attention. She slowed her car to a halt and looked toward the light. To her horror, bright flames shot from the second-floor window of Mr. Lee's home. Smoke billowed into the frigid night air. Dora had known Asher Lee since she was a little girl. She knew he had crippling arthritis that made walking difficult. If he was inside his home, he'd need help to get out.

She floored the accelerator and pulled into her driveway. Slipping and sliding across the ice, she rushed to her front door and thrust it open. "Mom, Dad, Tim, call 911. Mr. Lee's house is on fire. We need to get him out!"

. . . .

DISPATCHER: "Request for the fire department and first aid squad at 32 Ridge Road for an active structure fire."

I arrived at the first aid building as Mason Chapman was pulling the ambulance out onto the front apron. Mason worked as a mechanic at the local garage and used his knowledge and skills to help keep our ambulances in good working order.

Ted O'Malley, a member of our squad for five decades, was already sitting in the front passenger seat. In addition to being a retired electrician, he'd also spent many years working as a ranger for the national park system. He waved for me to get into the back of the ambulance.

I climbed in at the same time as Meg Potter. She'd recently switched from being a children's social worker in the hospital to working in private practice. As one of our squad's line officers, she helped efficiently manage our first aid calls. "I heard on my portable radio that it's really cooking."

Mason pulled out, along with our second ambulance, and followed the fire trucks to the scene. The ground was already icy, but I knew once the firefighters began hosing the burning house, flash freezing could make it even more treacherous. As we made our way to Ridge Road, I slipped on a pair of traction cleats over my boots. They'd provide me with some much-needed grip during the call.

. . . .

Angry flames crackled in the middle second-floor window of Asher Lee's home. Laura's father pounded on the front door. "I think I hear him calling for help."

"I've got this," Dora's brother, Tim, said. With a mighty heave, he pushed in the front door. Although smoke hung heavily in the air, the fire remained on the second floor. Together with their father, Dora and Tim rushed up the stairs.

They found Asher standing in the hallway at the top of the stairs, a thick haze of smoke surrounding him. Coughs racked his frail body. "Help me."

"It's going to be okay, Mr. Lee. We have you. Is anyone else in the house?" Dora asked.

Asher shook his head. The Winn family hoisted Asher into their arms and carried him down the flight of stairs. As they stepped outside, fire trucks began arriving.

"We'll take you to our house to get you out of the cold. Then I'll let the firefighters know what's going on," Mr. Winn said. Together they carried Mr. Lee several doors down to their own home.

. . . .

Mason parked our ambulance far enough away from the scene of the fire to leave room for the fire trucks. A network of firefighters aimed their hoses at the bright flames, beating back the blaze. The acrid stench of smoke filled the night air.

Pine Cove boasts a volunteer fire department consisting of many of the most talented and courageous men and women I know. If anyone could bring this fire under control, it was them.

"Hang tight for a minute. I'm going to see what's going on," Meg said. As she went to check with the command center, Ted and I gathered the equipment we might need, such as oxygen, our first aid bag, and our burn kit.

Meg returned a minute later. "Our patient's name is Asher Lee. He's in a neighbor's house," she said, pointing to a small Cape Cod–style home not far from where we were parked. "Fire Chief Watson said he inhaled smoke and needs to be checked out."

"I'll stay with the rig," Mason said.

A layer of slippery ice coated the road and sidewalk, and I was glad to be wearing my traction cleats. We worked our way to the neighbor's house and found Mr. Lee sitting in a high-back chair just inside the foyer. A young woman knelt next to him, holding his hand. A middle-aged couple and a young man also huddled around him. A hunter-green blanket was draped around his shoulders.

He was visibly shaking, which I figured was partly from the ordeal he'd just been through and partly from the blast of cold air we let in when we opened the front door. He appeared to be dazed. Black soot covered the area between his nose and upper lip. He'd benefit from a trip to the hospital to get thoroughly checked out.

Meg began assessing Asher's vital signs, while Ted wrote down what she said on our patient run sheet. "His blood pressure is elevated, 162 over 90. His pulse is 110, strong and regular. His respiratory rate is 20, and his pulse ox is 95 percent," Meg said. Pulse ox, short for pulse oximetry, measures the percentage of hemoglobin saturation ($SpO2$) in the blood. Normal is 98 to 100 percent if a person is breathing room air (as opposed to receiving supplemental oxygen). Asher's pulse ox reading was low, most likely due to his exposure to heavy smoke.

"I don't have any chest pain, but it's tough to get the air into my lungs," Asher said.

"Okay, I'm going to give you some oxygen to help with that." Meg placed him on high-flow oxygen via a non-rebreather mask. Non-rebreathers, which are for patients showing signs of hypoxia, deliver up to 95 percent oxygen at a flow rate of 10 to 15 liters per minute. Oxygen fills a reservoir bag that is attached to the mask by a one-way valve. It's called a non-rebreather mask because exhaled gas escapes through flapper valve ports at the cheek areas of the mask. The valves prevent patients from rebreathing exhaled gases.

Asher's past medical history included a heart attack (also known as a myocardial infarction or MI) two years prior, as well as severe osteoarthritis. "I need new hips and knees, but I've been pushing off surgery," he admitted.

Meg checked Asher's lung sounds with a stethoscope. "I hear some scattered rhonchi." Rhonchi are low-pitched breath sounds that resemble snoring. They occur when air tries to pass through bronchial tubes that contain fluid or mucus.

"I'm wearing cleats, so I'll get the stretcher while you finish his assessment," I said. A blast of icy air met me as I stepped outdoors. In the few short minutes that I had been inside with Asher, the firefighters had beaten the flames into submission.

I updated Mason about Asher Lee's condition as he helped me maneuver our stretcher across the icy pavement to the Winns' front porch. The spray from the fire hoses had turned the road into a virtual skating rink of dangerous black ice.

Chief Watson stepped inside after us to speak with Asher. "We've been able to contain much of the damage to the front bedroom. How are you feeling?"

"Better, thank you. I heard a loud bang and realized my TV was on fire. It's pretty old, and I had just been thinking about replacing it."

"That gives us a good starting point for our investigation," Chief Watson said.

Asher cast a grateful glance at Dora and her family. "I tried to call 911, but I couldn't get through. If you hadn't saved me, I hate to think what might've happened."

Dora squeezed his shoulder. "I'm so glad I got off work late. If I'd gotten home earlier, I may not have noticed anything unusual."

"Yes, it's incredibly fortunate," Chief Watson agreed. "Mr. Lee, do you have family in the area?"

Asher nodded. "Yes, I have a brother in town and a son who lives about a half hour away."

That made me feel better. At least Asher would have somewhere to stay while his house was getting repaired.

Chief Watson jotted down Asher's family members' phone numbers. "I don't want to keep you any longer. The squad is ready to take you to the hospital."

"I can't thank you and the other firefighters enough for all you've done. I'm not sure how I can repay you for all your help and kindness," Asher said.

"That's what we're here for. We're glad we could help," Chief Watson replied.

Asher's walker had been left behind in the blaze, so we lifted him onto our cot. We bundled him up with many blankets before rolling him out to the ambulance.

Thanks to the extraordinary courage and actions of the Winn family, Asher Lee survived the fire. God put the right people in the right place at the right time to rescue one of His own.

4

Surrounded by Love

My heart is glad and my tongue rejoices;
my body also will rest secure,
because you will not abandon me to the realm of the dead.

PSALM 16:9-10

Now that we've had lunch, I think it's time for a shower," Arnie Thompson suggested. He enjoyed working as a private duty aide for Declan Walters in the Little River Assisted Living Facility. He'd been taking care of Declan for the past six months and found him to be the perfect mix of cooperative and feisty.

Arnie knew when he took the job that Declan wasn't in the best of health. At 92 years young, he wasn't exactly what you'd call a "spring chicken." The last few years had been rough. Declan had had a heart attack the previous year and received an internal defibrillator. When the two first met, Declan had just begun chemotherapy for brain cancer.

"You think I need a shower? Okay, you're the boss. As long as it's nice and hot. You know how much I hate drafts," Declan said. Arnie walked by Declan's side from the combination bedroom/living area down a short hallway to the bathroom.

"Would you like to sit in the shower chair today?" Arnie asked.

"No, I prefer standing," Declan replied. He only used the shower chair when he felt fatigued. His family had bought it when he began chemotherapy treatments.

After about two minutes in the shower, Declan changed his mind. "On second thought, you can get me the chair. I'm starting to have trouble getting air in."

"I'll get your wheelchair, and we'll roll you out of here," Arnie said.

Declan's body grew limp. "I can't breathe."

Arnie grabbed Declan from behind and lowered him to the shower floor. "Call 911! I need help!" he yelled.

. . . .

DISPATCHER: "Request for first aid at the Little River Assisted Living Facility Room 12 for a 92-year-old male with difficulty breathing, currently in the shower and unable to get out."

I was driving toward a sporting goods store to take advantage of an after-Christmas sale when the call came. I lowered the speaker volume of my car radio so I could hear the dispatcher better. The Little River Assisted Living Facility was only a few blocks away in the opposite direction, so I did a U-turn and flipped on my blue emergency light.

As I pulled up to the facility, I noticed a Pine Cove patrol car was parked close by. I grabbed my first aid bag from my trunk. Fortunately, someone had propped open the front door. I ran inside and rushed along the hallway to Room 12.

When I entered, I found Officer Jack Endicott and a health aide lifting an unconscious man from the shower floor into a wheelchair.

"Andrea, if you roll the wheelchair out of here, Arnie and I will hold him and make sure he doesn't fall out," Officer Endicott said.

"Got it." I pulled the chair backward from the shower into the living room. I wasn't sure if our patient had a pulse or not. If he didn't, we'd have to start cardiopulmonary resuscitation (CPR) immediately.

"The patient's name is Declan Walters. This is his aide, Arnie. Declan began complaining of difficulty breathing and fell unconscious," Officer Endicott explained as we lifted him from the wheelchair onto the floor.

I knelt by Declan's head and slid my fingers onto his carotid artery. I detected a very faint pulse. However, he looked as though he could lose it at any moment. His face was stark white with a bluish undertone, and he didn't appear to be breathing adequately. "Let's use the bag valve mask." A bag valve mask (BVM) is used to provide positive-pressure ventilation to patients who are not breathing or who are not breathing adequately. A BVM can deliver up to 100 percent oxygen at 15 liters per minute with a reservoir bag.

Officer Endicott pulled the BVM out of his first aid bag. "I'll set it up."

Patsy, the competent and compassionate administrator of the facility, strode into the room. "Declan's a DNR." DNR stands for "do not resuscitate." In other words, if Declan went into cardiac arrest, we weren't allowed to do CPR.

Being a DNR changed our treatment plan. "Can we give him oxygen?" I asked.

"Yes, that would be fine. He has an oxygen machine at the far end of his bed. You can give him oxygen with a regular mask, but you can't assist his breathing with the BVM," Patsy said.

Declan's oxygen machine only provided up to six liters of oxygen via nasal cannula. Declan needed more than that. I placed a non-rebreather mask over his nose and mouth and adjusted the flow meter on our portable tank to 15 liters per minute.

"Let's lift him onto the bed," Officer Endicott suggested. "Since we can't do CPR, we can at least make him more comfortable." The four of us lifted him as a team, careful to support his head as we laid him on the bed.

Within seconds, Declan's eyes fluttered open. He struggled to sit up. "I need my clothes on!" he exclaimed.

A wave of relief washed over me. It appeared Declan was going to be okay after all. Rosy pink stained his cheeks, a welcome change from his earlier pallor.

Arnie raised the head of the bed and began dressing Declan. "You gave me a scare," he chided.

I fished a pulse oximeter out of my first aid bag. I placed the device on Declan's right index finger to determine his oxygen level, but I couldn't get a reading. I tried a different finger. No luck.

"Here, try mine," Officer Endicott suggested as he passed me an oximeter from his first aid kit. I slipped it on Declan's index finger. His reading was 80 percent. Dangerously low.

I placed a blood pressure cuff around Declan's upper arm. Unfortunately, after I pumped up the cuff and listened for Declan's pressure, I couldn't hear anything. *Not a good sign.*

I placed my index and middle fingers along the thumb side of Declan's wrist to check his pulse. "It's 59," I told Officer Endicott, who jotted it down on his notepad.

I patted Declan's shoulder. "As soon as the ambulance arrives, we'll take you to the hospital."

"You can't. He's on hospice," Patsy said. "I'll call the hospice nurse right away."

Normally, we aren't dispatched for hospice patients—those who are terminally ill and are receiving palliative comfort care. Emergency calls go to a hospice nurse rather than EMS (emergency medical services). Apparently, we had only ended up here this afternoon because of the extraordinary circumstances surrounding Declan's collapse in the shower. The news that Declan was on hospice further complicated matters.

Declan's breathing turned fast and shallow. His eyes grew wide, and he grasped Arnie's forearm.

Patsy stepped out of the room to call hospice and returned a few minutes later. "The hospice nurse is at least forty-five minutes away, maybe more. She said she's on her way here and doesn't want you to take Declan to the hospital. I realize you don't have to stay, but we don't have oxygen tanks here."

I squeezed Declan's hand. "We're going to stay." Perhaps we were there by accident, but we would stay. Volunteer first responders don't leave when someone needs them. It would be acting against our genetic makeup.

Declan's room had a sliding glass door that exited directly outdoors. I watched as Jose Sanchez parked our ambulance alongside the room, rather than in front of the facility. The rest of the volunteer EMS squad, including Ted O'Malley, Mason Chapman, Greg Turner, Meg Potter, and Sadie Martinez, soon stepped into the room. I explained to them Declan's condition.

Meg squeezed between the bedrail and wall on the far side of the bed. "I'll try once more to get a blood pressure reading." Still no luck.

Declan's anxiety increased, and he grew restless.

Ted, Mason, Greg, Meg, Sadie, Arnie, and I formed a human circle around Declan's bed. Sadie gently stroked his foot. Arnie patted his shoulder, while I stroked Declan's head.

A few minutes later, paramedics Arthur Williamson and Kennisha Smythe arrived from the hospital. Paramedics, who provide advanced life support (ALS), are paid employees of the hospital. Arthur and Kennisha, who have been partners for several years, are both experienced and knowledgeable.

"Technically, since he's a DNR on hospice, we really can't get involved," Arthur explained. "You need the hospice nurse."

Patsy frowned. "We're not sure when she's going to get here. She's at least forty-five minutes out. Do you have any suggestions?"

"Why don't you ask the hospice nurse if you can give him an Ativan?" Arthur asked. Ativan is a medication used to treat anxiety.

"Okay, I'll call her back and get an order to administer that." Pasty hurried out of the room to place the phone call.

Our squad members provided comforting words and touch to Declan until Patsy returned with an Ativan pill in her hand. "There's still no exact ETA on when the hospice nurse will arrive. I also spoke to Declan's family to let them know what's going on. His son lives in Virginia, and his daughter is in Maine. Fortunately, they just saw him a few days ago for Christmas."

"I'm afraid it's too late for Ativan," Kennisha said. "Declan's no longer alert enough to swallow a pill. Do you have it in an injectable form?"

Patsy shook her head. "I'll call the hospice nurse back."

"Do you have a hospice package here?" I asked. "Maybe something in the minifridge?" I knew from experience that patients on hospice often have a special kit in the refrigerator that includes medications such as morphine.

We searched Declan's fridge and room, but to no avail. At this point, 25 minutes had passed since we'd first arrived. Greg switched the portable oxygen tank to a fresh one.

"Let me try to get another set of vitals," Meg said. She placed the pulse oximeter on Declan's finger. "His pulse is 70, but his pulse ox is only 66 percent, even with the high-flow oxygen."

Arthur's radio crackled. "I'm sorry, but we have to leave now. We have another assignment."

"Thanks for your help," I murmured. I was grateful for their input. Now, we were on our own.

Declan's pulse ox reading no longer registered. His gaze became unseeing. He closed his eyes. His breathing rate slowed. He began slipping away.

"Your family called," I told him. "They're so happy they saw you at Christmas. They're sending all their love." I gently stroked the top of Declan's head as I spoke. Although he was now unconscious, I hoped he heard what I was saying.

Patsy rejoined us. "I'm sorry to say there's still no arrival time for hospice. I'm working on finding out if there's something else we can do for him until the nurse gets here."

"I don't think she's going to make it on time. He's going to pass soon," I said.

"Oh no! Poor Declan." Patsy blinked back tears. I could tell she cared greatly for him. "I'm going to call his family again. I told them he wasn't feeling well but not that he might expire. I'll call back the hospice nurse too." She stroked Declan's arm before leaving the room.

Declan's complexion turned gray. His breathing switched to agonal respirations, which are ineffective, gasping breaths.

We took turns speaking soothingly to Declan. Since his loved ones lived many miles away, we became his surrogate family. We poured love on Declan like syrup on a buttermilk pancake. There wasn't an inch of him that wasn't covered. We engulfed him with a giant blanket of human love.

Declan took his last breath and transitioned peacefully from his earthly life to his eternal life with Christ.

I think most of us contemplate at some point or another what our ending will be like. Will we be young? Old? Alone? With family? Will we be staring at the pearly gates of heaven? Have we accepted Christ as our Savior?

On that day, Jesus granted us the opportunity to assist in a way first responders normally don't. We're usually in the business of saving lives rather than providing a loving send-off.

Despite the sadness of the situation, I felt privileged to be with Declan in his final hour on earth. And I felt blessed to witness an amazing display of kindness, patience, and love from my fellow squad members and the staff at Little River Assisted Living Facility.

5

Rock Bottom

Be strong and take heart,
all you who hope in the LORD.

PSALM 31:24

The temptation was almost too much to bear. Riley Benton tried not to think about the bags of heroin she had safely tucked away in the underwear drawer of her dresser. She tried to ignore how much she wanted to shoot up. An unimaginably intense craving consumed her. She tried to distract herself by thinking about something else. Anything else. But the yearning made it impossible. All she could think about was how good she would feel if she could have some. She knew deep down she wouldn't be able to resist the urge forever. Sooner or later, she'd give in to the desire. She broke out in a cold sweat at the thought.

Riley was only 23 years old, and she'd already been in and out of rehab more times than she cared to admit. In fact, she'd just gotten out of a place four weeks ago. She had done well while she was there. She'd begun to feel like she could truly conquer her addiction.

The day Riley was discharged, she vowed to clean up her act and start fresh. Her parents helped get her a part-time job scooping ice cream. It wasn't much, but it was a start. Her uncle was even letting her stay rent-free in his apartment while he was overseas. "Just until you get back on your feet," he'd said.

Now, Riley felt drawn to the bedroom. She rested her arms across the top of the dresser and stared out the bedroom window. Beautiful pink and white impatiens formed a circular border around a large oak tree in the center court of the apartment complex. The sun was setting, casting long shadows across the courtyard. She envied the robin that grabbed a worm and flew away. Free. Unencumbered.

Riley heard the front door open and then click shut. She regretted mentioning to one of her friends that she had a stash of heroin. What if they talked her into using it?

. . . .

DISPATCHER: "Request for first aid at Pine Cove Apartments, building 1, apartment E, for a possible overdose."

I flipped my laptop shut, jumped to my feet, and slipped on a pair of sneakers. Two minutes later, I hopped into the ambulance's passenger seat as Jessie Barnes started the engine.

DISPATCHER: "Update: suspected heroin overdose. You have one EMT at the scene who can ride to the hospital."

"We're in service," Jessie replied. He flipped on the lights and sirens. Just before we reached the railroad crossing, the gates came down. "We're going to be delayed a few minutes waiting for the train," he updated dispatch.

A short while later, we pulled up in front of a red-brick apartment complex. I spotted fellow squad member Helen McGuire's car parked close by. Several patrol cars were also parked in front of building 1. I knew from experience that apartment E was on the second floor, with a covered outdoor staircase.

Jessie and I grabbed our first aid gear and rushed along a concrete sidewalk lined with robust variegated hosta plants. Two potted pink geraniums, which looked like they could use a good watering, decorated the apartment's porch steps. We hastened up the stairs and found the door to apartment E flung wide open. "We're back here," Helen called to us.

Jessie and I followed the sound of Helen's voice to the rear of the apartment and turned right into a crowded bedroom. A young woman with shoulder-length dark-blond hair lay unresponsive on the floor.

Officer Brad Sims knelt next to the patient's head. Competent and professional, Officer Sims had been with the Pine Cove Police Department for five years. An imposing figure at six foot three, he towered over many people. I felt he was on track to achieve the rank of sergeant within the next couple of years. "Riley Benton appears to have had a heroin overdose. Her pupils are constricted. So far, we've given her one dose of naloxone."

Naloxone is an opioid antagonist. Sometimes people call it Narcan, which is a brand name of the generic form of naloxone. If it's administered in time, it will completely reverse the effects of an opioid overdose. In the field, police and EMS most commonly administer it through an intranasal route (that is, into a patient's nasal passages).

I studied Riley's appearance. She was unconscious, and her breathing was slow, shallow, and erratic. The opioid overdose triad includes pinpoint pupils, unconsciousness, and respiratory depression. Riley had all three signs.

"We'll have to hit her with a second dose if she doesn't improve in the next minute or two," Sergeant Derrick Flint said. Hardworking and meticulous, Sergeant Flint had been with the department for a decade.

"Her respiratory rate is slow. Let's bag her," Jessie said. He pulled the bag valve mask out of our bag, attached it to a portable oxygen tank, and passed it to Helen.

Helen pulled the non-rebreather mask off Riley's face and began assisting her ventilations with the BVM. "You can give me a nasal airway too."

A young man with shaggy brown hair hovered near the doorway. He glanced back over his shoulder, appearing anxious to leave. Since

I was writing down information on our clipboard, I stepped closer to him to find out what was going on before he bolted.

He began, "A friend of mine called me and told me to come check on Riley. I found her on the floor, all curled up into a ball, lying on her side. I couldn't wake her up. I called 911 right away."

"Does your friend have a history of drug abuse?" I asked.

"Yeah, she just got out of rehab a month ago for using heroin. She's been trying to clean up." He inched closer to the doorway, as if planning his exit.

"Don't worry," I assured him. "You can't get in trouble for calling 911. Riley won't get in trouble either." The Good Samaritan Drug Overdose Act provides immunity to those who call 911. By providing legal protection, it encourages people to seek medical attention for drug overdose victims instead of failing to act out of fear of prosecution. In this case, it allowed Riley's friend to call for help on her behalf. Neither Riley nor her friend could be charged in relation to drug offenses.

At that point, Sergeant Flint plunged naloxone into Riley's nasal passage. "I'm administering a second dose right now."

"Her pulse is 56 and irregular," Jessie said. I turned toward him and jotted down the number on the call sheet. When I turned back around, Riley's friend had vanished.

"The Narcan is kicking in. I think she's starting to wake up," Officer Sims said.

Riley's breathing became stronger and more regular. Helen switched her back to the non-rebreather mask and made sure it was cranked to 15 liters per minute.

Riley opened her eyes and blinked rapidly several times, obviously trying to figure out what was happening and why a bunch of strangers were surrounding her. She yanked off the mask and began sitting up.

"It's okay, Riley," Helen said. "You overdosed, and we just gave you naloxone. It would be better if you kept the oxygen mask on," she added as she guided it back toward Riley's face.

After we resuscitate a victim of a drug overdose, it's rare for him or her to thank us—at least right away. Naloxone causes side effects such as body aches, trembles, diarrhea, increased heart rate, fever, runny nose, nausea, restlessness, irritability, and stomach cramps. Not exactly the kind of symptoms that put people in a good mood. Not to mention the fact that we ruin the victim's high by administering naloxone. We take great care in case our patient becomes combative.

Riley scowled and pushed Officer Sims's arm. "Get away from me. I'm fine. I want everyone to leave."

Even if a victim of drug overdose wakes up, we normally still transport him or her to the hospital. The effects of the naloxone can wear off, causing the patient to fall back into respiratory depression or even respiratory arrest. It's best if they are evaluated by an emergency department physician. In addition, we hope the person will be amenable to transferring from the hospital to a drug rehabilitation facility.

Helen tried once more to bring the oxygen mask closer to Riley's face, but Riley swatted it away. "I said no!"

"Your friend called us to come help you," Jessie explained.

Riley looked around the room. "I don't see anyone. What friend?" she asked suspiciously.

"He said his name was Randy," Officer Sims said. "Another friend of yours called him to come check on you. If he hadn't come here right away, you wouldn't be alive right now."

"I just spoke to your father," Sergeant Flint added. "He's going to meet us at the emergency department."

Riley stopped struggling and grew quiet as the officers' words slowly penetrated through her post-overdose fog. "Okay. I'll go."

I slipped downstairs to get our stair chair. When I stepped back into the room, Riley was still sitting on the floor.

"Let's help you up onto your feet and into this chair," Jessie said. He and Sergeant Flint assisted her.

"The medics just arrived on scene," Officer Sims said. "I'll tell them we'll meet them in the ambulance."

We carefully moved Riley down the stairs and transferred her onto our stretcher while paramedics Arthur Williamson and Kennisha Smythe set up their equipment in the back of our ambulance. I gave them our patient report.

"There are some bad batches of heroin out there right now. There could have been fentanyl mixed in," Arthur commented. Fentanyl is a synthetic opioid that is much more powerful than morphine. It's sometimes added to heroin to increase its potency. Unsuspecting users can easily die if they don't realize the heroin is cut with fentanyl.

Helen and Jessie lifted the stretcher into the back of the ambulance. "I'll take over driving," Helen said. Jessie climbed into the back with me. Kennisha stepped out to drive the paramedic ambulance to the hospital, while Arthur began an assessment of Riley. He placed electrodes on her chest to perform a 12-lead ECG (electrocardiogram). Fortunately, Riley's heart rhythm was unremarkable.

"Her blood pressure is now 124 over 82, and the pulse is 94," I said. Her vital signs were returning to normal.

Riley frowned. "This should never have happened. I just got out of rehab four weeks ago, and I've been doing good. Sure, I've been tempted, but I haven't given in. That is, until today."

Jessie slipped a pulse oximeter onto Riley's index finger. "Don't beat yourself up. You have a fresh start."

"How much did you take today?" Arthur asked.

Riley sighed. "One bag, I think. I usually have one or two a day, but I haven't had any since I got out of rehab."

Addiction is a brutal illness. Substance abuse is characterized by a strong desire to take opioids, a lack of control over opioid use, and ongoing use despite harmful consequences. Some addicts place a higher priority on opioid use than work, family, and other activities. They suffer withdrawal reactions if they try to discontinue using the drugs.

Although Riley initially seemed angry, I think she was frustrated with herself for relapsing. I suppose that sometimes people need to hit rock bottom before they can begin climbing back up.

I reflected that it was a blessing her friend came to check on her that day. If more time had passed, it would have been too late to save her. I knew she had a supportive family who would be by her side to help her make a fresh start. Riley would most likely have ups and downs ahead of her. I prayed that with strength from the Lord, she would be able to overcome her addiction and live a happy and productive life.

. . . .

Six years later

"I'm sorry, but I'm going to have to leave," Officer Sims said. "I have another call. Are you going to be okay with just the two of you?"

"It's okay. We'll manage," Jessie replied. Jessie and I were on a first aid call at Pine Cove Apartments for an elderly male with leg pain. We'd have to bring him down the flight of stairs using the stair chair. Normally, we have someone back us up when we go down the stairs. And our patient was a big guy. Now, Jessie and I would have to manage on our own. I didn't relish the prospect.

We rolled our patient out of his apartment toward the stairs. Just at that moment, the door to apartment E opened, and a stylishly dressed young woman stepped out. She looked vaguely familiar, but I couldn't quite place her.

She stepped closer to us. "Hi, Mr. Boswell. Are you okay?"

"Well, I've been better," he replied. "These nice folks are taking me to the hospital. My legs are really bothering me."

Something about the woman's voice sparked a memory. I looked at her more closely. Suddenly, I realized it was Riley Benton, the girl who had overdosed on heroin years ago. I was pleased to see how well she looked. It appeared that she'd cleaned up her act.

"Is it just the two of you? Would you like a hand?" Riley asked.

I smiled. "That would be great, thank you. Could you back me up when we go down the stairs?"

Riley stepped behind me, keeping her hand on my low back as we slowly worked our way down the staircase. Once we got to the bottom, she stood next to our stretcher while we pivoted Mr. Boswell from the chair to the cot.

A glow of warmth infused my heart. Six years ago, I had helped carry Riley down these very stairs in the stair chair. Now, she was returning the favor.

"I recognize you from when you helped me years ago," Riley said softly. "Thanks for all you did for me that day. I'm doing much better now. I've got a good job, and I have a nice boyfriend."

"Congratulations. I'm so glad to hear it. You made my day." We exchanged a quick hug.

Riley patted Mr. Boswell's shoulder. "I'll look after your apartment while you're in the hospital."

Riley is a shining example of how someone can turn her life around. I prayed she would enjoy a long, happy, and successful life with God by her side.

6

Anything for Ice Cream

Be completely humble and gentle; be patient,
bearing with one another in love.

EPHESIANS 4:2

> **DISPATCHER:** "Request for first aid at 720 Daisy Drive, apartment 2, for a 46-year-old male with chest pain."

It was just past two in the morning. I roused from a deep sleep, jumped out of bed, and slipped on my jeans and sneakers. I swished a bit of mint fluoride rinse around in my mouth and hurried out the door, heading to our first aid building.

I'm on the Thursday night crew. Since we're a volunteer rescue squad, we have dedicated crews on call Monday through Thursday from 10:00 p.m. to 6:00 a.m. That way, we ensure an EMS crew will always be available to respond. On weekend nights, it's "all hands on deck." That means whoever can respond does. Of course, if there is a large-scale call on a weeknight other than our designated crew night, like a car accident or house fire, we all try to respond.

On my crew night, I usually say a quick prayer that there are no calls. I admit, it's not just because I hope everyone in my town stays safe and healthy. I also pray because I want to enjoy a good night's sleep.

As soon as I arrived at the squad building and saw I was the first one there, I pulled the ambulance out onto the front apron. Soon, my fellow crew members Mason Chapman and Ted O'Malley arrived. I flipped on our emergency lights and called us in service, all the while suppressing a shiver. It was a chilly spring night, and I was glad I'd grabbed my hoodie on the way out. Mist rolled across the roadway, so I flipped on the windshield wipers.

"Pull around back of the apartment complex," Dispatcher Jerome Franklin said.

Officer Vinnie McGovern met us at the front door of the apartment. Officer McGovern, a former corrections officer in South Carolina, relocated to Pine Cove to be closer to family. He'd been a member of the police force for more than a dozen years. "Jamie Boyle is 46 years old," he informed us. "He just moved in a few days ago. According to his aide, Jamie was having trouble falling asleep tonight. Then he began complaining of severe chest pain, which he rates ten out of ten."

It sounded serious. Could he be having a heart attack? "Are the medics coming?"

"Yes, they have a ten-minute ETA," Officer McGovern replied as he led us through a dimly lit living room toward the bedroom. Stacks of boxes lined the hallway. It looked like Jamie was still in the process of unpacking. We'd probably need to slide some of the boxes out of the way to get him out of the apartment.

A middle-aged male with thinning brown hair sat on the edge of his bed. He pulled downward on the edges of his plain white T-shirt.

"Hi, I'm Mason with the Pine Cove First Aid Squad. Can you tell me what's going on tonight?"

Jamie looked down at his toes. "I've got chest pain."

"On a scale of one to ten, with ten being the worst pain, how would you describe your pain?" Mason asked.

"Ten."

Mason stepped closer to Jamie. "Does it radiate into your arms or stay in your chest?"

Jamie tapped his chest in response.

Ted handed a blood pressure cuff to Mason and slipped the pulse oximeter onto Jamie's finger. I noticed Jamie's color looked good. He wasn't pale or diaphoretic (sweaty), which can be indicators of cardiac problems.

"His blood pressure is 112 over 82, and his pulse is 64. His pulse ox is 99 percent on room air," Mason said.

I jotted the information down on our patient call sheet. Then I noticed a young man wearing navy-blue scrubs standing in the far corner of the room. I wondered if he was Jamie's caretaker. As Mason continued with the patient assessment, I stepped toward the gentleman. "Are you Jamie's aide?"

He nodded. "Yes, I'm Marv."

"Does he have any medical problems?" I asked.

"This is my first day with Jamie. I'm not sure, but I think he has a history of chest pain. Let me get you his list of medications." He stepped out of the bedroom.

I took a closer look at Jamie. He didn't look like a person who has ten-out-of-ten chest pain. Something didn't quite add up.

Just then, paramedics Ty Fleming and Paula Pritchard arrived. Ty was currently taking prerequisite classes to go to medical school. He planned to one day become an emergency room physician. Paula was his new partner. She'd switched from a career as a preschool teacher to being a paramedic.

I stepped back several steps to give the medics room to work. Ty hooked up Jamie to a 12-lead ECG, while Paula began documenting. I relayed the information we'd gathered thus far.

A few minutes later, Marv returned with a handwritten list of Jamie's medications. I noticed a few were related to conditions like anxiety and depression.

Ty printed out a strip of Jamie's ECG reading. "Your heart rhythm is normal. There's nothing I can see on your ECG that shows your chest pain is coming from your heart. What did you have for dinner?"

Rather than answer for himself, Jamie looked at Marv.

"He had chicken nuggets, mashed potatoes, and green beans," Marv replied.

Ty performed several more tests on Jamie and assessed his lung sounds. "There's nothing we can treat. We're going to release you to the BLS unit." BLS stands for basic life support, meaning EMTs—as opposed to paramedics, who offer advanced life support (ALS).

Jamie shrugged. "I've got chest pain. I need to go to the hospital."

"We're going to take you to Bakersville Hospital," I said. The paramedics departed, and we helped Jamie onto our stretcher. After we loaded him into the ambulance, I drove us to the emergency department.

Ted gave our report to veteran triage nurse Maggie Summers. Organized and efficient, Maggie helped ensure the ED ran smoothly.

I realized that during our entire time with Jamie, his condition remained unchanged. I'll admit, I was curious as to the source of his chest pain.

By the time I returned to bed, I had only three more hours until I had to get up for work. I closed my eyes and hoped I'd fall asleep quickly.

. . . .

A few days later

I soaked up the warm afternoon sun during a bike ride around the lake. Afterward, I was parking my bike in our garage when my pager went off.

DISPATCHER: "Request for first aid at 720 Daisy Drive, apartment 2, for a 46-year-old male with difficulty breathing."

I biked over to the first aid building and met up with Helen McGuire and Alec Waters. Alec was the one who had convinced me to start volunteering with the first aid squad. Now, he was studying to become a veterinarian. Intelligent and kind, he'd make a great vet one day.

"The patient's name is Jamie," I explained as Helen drove us to the scene. "He just moved into the apartment a few days ago. We had him for chest pain the other night. I'm not sure what was going on with him. The paramedics didn't find anything wrong related to his heart and released him to us."

"He probably didn't get admitted to the hospital if he's already back home," Alec noted.

When we arrived, we found Jamie sitting on a sofa in the living room. Alec introduced himself. "We were told you're having trouble breathing. Can you tell me what made you call us today?"

"I'm having trouble breathing. I want to go to the hospital," Jamie replied.

I noticed Jamie was speaking in full sentences without difficulty. That's a sign he wasn't acutely short of breath.

"Hi again," I said as I strapped a blood pressure cuff around Jamie's upper arm. "What did the doctor think your chest pain was due to the other night?"

Jamie shrugged. "I don't know."

At this point, Marv stepped forward. "They didn't find anything wrong and sent him home a few hours later."

"His blood pressure is 112 over 62, and his pulse is 64 and regular," I said. "His respiratory rate is 12, and his pulse ox reading is 100 percent on room air." Although Jamie reported he was having respiratory distress, his vital signs didn't back up the claim. Helen jotted down the information on our run sheet.

The same team of paramedics who had responded to Jamie a few days ago, Ty and Paula, arrived. They did a thorough assessment and, once again, they couldn't find anything wrong with him that they could treat. "We're going to release him to you," Paula said.

Jamie didn't seem fazed that the medics couldn't find a cause for his reported breathing difficulties. "Let's go to the hospital now."

When we arrived at the hospital, I gave our report to Maggie. "I remember him," she said. "He was just here the other day."

"Yes, that's right. He was discharged, and now he's back complaining of difficulty breathing."

We said goodbye to Jamie. He seemed content on the hospital stretcher. If he'd had difficulty breathing earlier, the issue certainly seemed gone now.

Three days later

I finished my shift at work as a physical therapist and checked to see what calls I had missed by replaying my pager. There was one for "720 Daisy Drive, apartment 2, for a 46-year-old male with stomach pains." Jamie again.

. . . .

A week later

DISPATCHER: "Request for first aid at 720 Daisy Drive, apartment 2, for a 46-year-old male with a psychiatric emergency."

It was just before midnight. I'd already been sleeping for a couple hours. I met up with Jessie Barnes and Ted O'Malley at the first aid building.

"We had this guy a week ago with a stomachache. He seemed fine though," Jessie commented.

"I had him for chest pain, and then a few days later with difficulty breathing. He didn't really seem in distress either time," I said.

When we arrived, Jamie was sitting on his front patio with his aide, Marv. Jamie didn't make eye contact with us. Instead, he stared up at the clouds.

Officer McGovern stood next to them. "Jamie told Marv that he wanted to harm himself, so he called 911 for help."

This time, Jamie didn't complain of chest pains or difficulty breathing. He rubbed the palms of his hands on his thighs. "I want to go to the hospital."

"Is something troubling you? Did you tell Marv you wanted to harm yourself?" Ted asked.

Jamie shrugged. "Let's go to the hospital."

"Let's check his vital signs in the ambulance on the way to the hospital," Jessie suggested.

The three of us brought Jamie to the ED. Not surprisingly, it was an unremarkable trip. Soon I was happily tucked back in my bed, and thoughts of Jamie faded away.

. . . .

The next morning

> **DISPATCHER:** "Request for first aid at 720 Daisy Drive, apartment 2, for a 46-year-old male with an unknown medical emergency."

"Let me guess. Chest pain, difficulty breathing, stomach pain, or a psychiatric crisis," I said, climbing into the passenger seat next to Helen.

Helen grimaced. "It seems like we're going to this apartment a lot."

We parked by the curb in front of the apartment building. Sergeant Derrick Flint met us by the ambulance. "Sorry to bring you out. I tried to talk him out of it. He has a substitute aide today, and the aide said they haven't really hit it off."

I raised my eyebrows. "So they called 911?"

The new aide met us at the front door. "I don't think Jamie cares for me. I get the impression he wanted me to call 911 just so he could get away from me. He knows if he says that he wants to kill himself, he has to go to the ED."

"Well, there's a good reason to go the emergency room. Escapism," I whispered to Helen.

We took Jamie to the ED as requested. I was starting to feel like I was spending more time with Jamie than with my own family.

A few days later

We took Jamie to the hospital again.

The next day

And again.

Two days later

And yet again.

. . . .

One week later

> **DISPATCHER:** "Request for first aid at 720 Daisy Drive, apartment 2, for a 51-year-old male with a leg laceration."

I met Jessie and Alec at the squad building. "They got his age wrong. Jamie is 46, not 51," Jessie said.

When we arrived at the apartment, we discovered that the first aid call was, in fact, for Jamie's roommate. He'd tripped on a coffee table and cut his right lower leg. It looked like he might need a few stitches.

Jamie sat on the sofa and watched with great interest. I hoped watching us didn't give him the idea that he wanted to join his roommate and go to the ED as well.

One hour later

We were just driving back into town after dropping off Jamie's roommate at Bakersville Hospital when another call came.

> **DISPATCHER:** "Request for first aid at 720 Daisy Drive, apartment 2, for a 46-year-old male who is depressed."

I stifled a groan. "I just knew he was going to ask to go to the hospital."

"We could have saved ourselves an hour and just taken them both at the same time," Alec said.

When we arrived at the apartment once again, I spotted Jamie sitting on his front patio. When he saw our ambulance pull in, he stood up and shuffled to the road to meet us. "I want to go to the hospital."

So, within a short hour, we had taken both occupants of 720 Daisy Drive to the ED.

. . . .

A few days later

> **DISPATCHER:** "Request for first aid at 720 Daisy Drive, apartment 2, for a 46-year-old male with chest pain."

It was a few hours before my crew night, which officially starts at 10:00 p.m. I was almost relieved that we were having the first aid call for Jamie now, before it ruined my sleep. I figured if we dropped him off at 8:00 p.m., we should be good for the rest of the night.

I was wrong.

The next morning, 4:30 a.m.

> **DISPATCHER:** "Request for first aid at 720 Daisy Drive, apartment 2, for a 46-year-old male with chest pain."

I couldn't believe it. Well, actually, I could believe it. But I didn't want to believe it. Another night of lost sleep. I prayed to God for patience. I knew Jamie suffered from mental illness. But to be fair, I was beginning to suffer from sleep deprivation.

The rest of my (sleepy) crewmates met me at the squad building.

Ted shook his head in disbelief. "Jamie couldn't have been home for more than an hour."

When we stepped into Jamie's apartment a short while later, Officer McGovern said, "I'm so sorry."

"It's okay. It's not your fault," I replied.

Not surprisingly, Jamie's chest pain didn't seem authentic. "Why did you call us back so soon?" Ted asked.

Jamie shrugged. "The nurse said to come back if my pain got worse." We took Jamie to the ED as requested.

. . . .

The next day

> **DISPATCHER:** "Request for first aid at 720 Daisy Drive, apartment 2, for a 46-year-old male with a medical emergency."

I glanced at my alarm clock. It was 3:05 a.m. It wasn't my crew night. With relief, I rolled over and went back to sleep.

. . . .

We took Jamie to the hospital a dozen times over the next month. One Friday evening, while we were on a first aid call for him, Helen asked the police if social services could do anything to help.

"We're a volunteer squad. He's straining our resources," I lamented.

"We're working on it," Officer McGovern replied.

On the way to the hospital, I said, "Jamie, we have six members out of town at training this weekend. Please do not call us unless you absolutely, truly need us."

Jamie nodded. I hoped he understood what I was saying.

The next afternoon

> **DISPATCHER:** "Request for first aid at 720 Daisy Drive, apartment 2, for a 46-year-old male crisis patient."

I guess Jamie didn't take my plea seriously. We took him to Bakersville Hospital. Again.

. . . .

"I just counted. We've taken Jamie to the hospital more than thirty times in the last three months," Ted said.

I sighed. "Social services told the police department that Jamie's moving at the end of this week, but I'll believe it when I see it." It seemed too good to be true.

Over the next few weeks, we had a noticeable lack of calls for Jamie. Had he truly moved after all?

"Social services said he was diagnosed with attention-seeking disorder," Jessie said. "One of the police officers told me Jamie officially moved last week."

I hoped he would receive the care he needed. And I looked forward to some uninterrupted nights of sleep.

. . . .

Three months later

DISPATCHER: "Request for first aid at 720 Daisy Drive, apartment 2, for a 46-year-old male with chest pain."

I woke up with a start. No way. Jamie had moved. How was it possible? Was I dreaming? Was it a nightmare? I pinched myself. Ouch! No, I wasn't dreaming. I dragged myself out of bed and met my crew members at the squad building.

The next day

We had another call for Jamie.

The second day

Another call. I was at work, so I missed it.

The third day

Another call. I missed this one too.

The fourth day

Another call for Jamie.

The fifth day

Yes, of course. Another call for Jamie.

> **DISPATCHER:** "Request for first aid at 720 Daisy Drive, apartment 2, for a 46-year-old male with a medical emergency."

Alec, Jessie, and I found Jamie sitting on the edge of his bed, rocking back and forth.

"What can we do for you tonight?" Alec asked.

"I need to go to the hospital. I need ice cream," Jamie said.

"Excuse me?" I asked. *Please, someone tell me I misheard him. Please tell me Jamie didn't really call us here this evening because he wants ice cream.*

Jamie scowled. "I want ice cream."

Marv smiled apologetically. "Jamie often has ice cream for dessert, but we ran out. I told him I could go to the store tomorrow to get more."

"Jamie, calling 911 is for emergencies," I said. "We cannot take you to the ED for ice cream. I don't even think they have ice cream there."

Jamie rocked faster. "Yes, they do. Chocolate and vanilla in little containers. I had it there a few nights ago. I want to go to the hospital."

"We cannot take you to the hospital because you want ice cream," Alec said firmly. "Your blood pressure and heart rate are fine. There is no reason for you to go to the ED. You can have ice cream tomorrow."

Jamie smirked. "I have chest pain." He pointed to the center of his chest. "Now you have to take me to the hospital."

"Jamie's learned that if he says he has chest pain or difficulty breathing, he gets to go to the hospital," Marv explained.

We gave up arguing and drove Jamie to the Bakersville ED.

I found Maggie sitting behind her desk.

"What brings Jamie here this evening?" the triage nurse asked. "Chest pain? Psychiatric emergency?"

"Jamie needs ice cream," I said, making sure to keep my tone completely neutral.

Maggie raised one eyebrow. "Please tell me you are joking."

"He would prefer vanilla and chocolate swirl," I said with a deadpan expression.

. . . .

Through Jamie's antics, God helped teach me the importance of empathy and understanding. Over the first few months of first aid calls for Jamie, there were times I felt frustrated and even annoyed. God responded to my prayers for patience and hope for a solution for our dilemma by sustaining us through this trying experience.

Jamie moved away for good a short time after that. I bet Marv made sure to keep the freezer well-stocked with ice cream.

7

Clamp It

*This day I call the heavens and the earth as
witnesses against you that I have set before you
life and death, blessings and curses. Now choose
life, so that you and your children may live.*

DEUTERONOMY 30:19

Rory Clayton paused momentarily from cutting a stack of lumber with a circular saw. He was thrilled to have landed this construction job. Renovating this house would take several months and would provide a much-needed cash infusion into his bank account.

Having a steady paycheck had become more important to Rory. His sister, a single parent, bravely battled breast cancer for years. Then, four weeks ago, she'd succumbed to the disease. She'd left behind two sons, an eight-year-old and a ten-year-old—Rory's nephews.

The boys were currently in foster care. Rory was trying to save enough money to take custody of them. The judge had said certain things needed to be in place before Rory could have the boys. Rory was determined to work hard and do whatever it took to provide a good home for his sister's kids.

As Rory resumed cutting, he thought he heard someone call his name. Distracted, he looked up. The circular saw slipped from his hand. The jagged teeth of the saw ripped through his jeans and thermal underwear and cut deeply into his right upper thigh.

"Help!" Rory yelled as he collapsed to the ground, clutching his leg. Bright red blood soaked his clothes, forming a puddle beneath him.

Rory's coworkers, including a man named Joey, rushed to help him. "Call 911," Joey directed as he pulled off his coat, sweatshirt, and thermal top. He tore off the arms of the thermal shirt and tied them around Rory's upper thigh to create a tourniquet. "You're going to be okay. Help is on the way."

. . . .

That day the afternoon sun shone brightly following several days of heavy rain, but it did little to warm the frigid January air.

DISPATCHER: "Request for first aid at 452 Hudson Avenue for a man with a severe leg laceration from a saw."

I'd just returned home from my job as a physical therapist and was changing out of my work clothes when I received the call. Before I could reach the first aid building, the ambulance called in service. So instead of turning left, I made a quick right and headed to the accident location. I pulled up behind Officer Brad Sims's police car.

My gaze swept over the scene. I'd driven by the large Victorian numerous times over the past several weeks and knew it was undergoing a renovation. I spotted a cluster of men huddled together on the side porch. To get to them, I trudged through a giant sea of deep brown mud (knowing that my brand-new white sneakers would never be the same). Since the home was undergoing construction, there were no steps to get onto the porch. Instead, there was a foot-wide plank of plywood serving as a ramp. I hoped it would hold my weight. I didn't want to misstep and fall into the mud.

"This is Rory Clayton," Officer Sims explained to me. "He's 38 years old. The circular saw got away on him and caught his right thigh." He pointed to the young man who stood next to him. "When I got here, Joey had already applied a tourniquet made from his shirt." A tourniquet is a device, typically a tightly encircling bandage, used to control bleeding by temporarily stopping the flow of blood through a large artery in a person's arm or leg. It's only used for serious bleeding emergencies.

"It was really spurting. I hope I did the right thing," Joey said.

"You certainly did. That was quick thinking on your part," Officer Sims replied.

Rory was sitting in a white plastic lawn chair. Another was set up facing him, and his right leg was resting on it. Blood had soaked through the cloth tourniquet. Officer Sims placed him on high-flow oxygen via a non-rebreather mask.

Although Rory had lost a considerable amount of blood, he remained conscious and alert. When people lose a large amount of blood or bodily fluids, they can go into shock. If a person is in shock, the tissues in the body don't receive enough oxygen and nutrients to allow the cells to function. If untreated, this eventually leads to cellular death, progressing to organ failure, and finally whole-body failure and death.

There are numerous types of shock. Hypovolemic shock occurs when there is an inadequate amount of fluid or volume in the circulatory system. Bleeding emergencies can result in hemorrhagic hypovolemic shock—which was a risk for Rory.

Our ambulance arrived then, and Ted O'Malley and Archie Harris joined us on the porch. Archie had retired from a long career with the state government. He'd been volunteering with our rescue squad for decades.

Rory closed his eyes and tightly clutched the armrests of the chair. "I can't believe this is happening. It hurts so bad."

"How would you rate your pain on a scale of zero to ten, if ten is the worst pain and zero is no pain at all?" I asked.

Rory grimaced. "It's at least an eight out of ten."

I placed a bulky sterile trauma dressing over the wound. The homemade tourniquet had slowed the flow greatly, but the wound was still bleeding. "We're going to take you to the hospital. It's a regional trauma center." I held the dressing in place while Ted secured it with sterile conforming gauze.

Archie placed a backboard on the porch next to Rory. "I think this will be the best option to lift him safely off the porch."

While Archie and Ted prepared the backboard straps, I took a set of vital signs. "The blood pressure is 160 over 110; pulse is 72, strong and regular; respiratory rate is 18; and pulse ox is 98 percent." I thought perhaps his blood pressure was elevated due to pain and fear.

"The paramedics should be arriving within two to three minutes," Officer Sims said.

"That gives us enough time to get Rory out of the cold and into our ambulance," Archie noted. We lifted Rory from the lawn chair to the backboard. I took great care to support his leg and make sure it didn't get jostled. Officer Sims and Ted climbed down the plank and stood on the ground near the porch. We slid the backboard off the edge of the porch into their waiting arms. Once we loaded Rory into the ambulance, we removed him from the backboard.

The paramedics' ambulance parked behind us. A minute later, Rose Anderson and William Moore entered our rig with their equipment. Rose had been a paramedic in Iowa for many years before getting married and relocating to our region. William, a former accountant, had grown tired of the corporate world and switched to the medical field a few years prior to this time.

Archie opened the side door. "I'll move to the driver's seat and give you room to work."

William introduced himself and Rose to Rory. "I'm going to start an intravenous line." That way, he'd be able to provide fluids if Rory began to go into shock.

Rose passed me a pair of scissors. "Can you cut off his pants?" Now that we were inside the warm ambulance, we needed to be better able to visualize Rory's wound.

Ted switched the oxygen line from the portable tank to the onboard ambulance unit while I cut through Rory's jeans and thermals.

After William established an IV line, Rose stepped out to drive their ambulance. "You can start rolling," Ted called to Archie.

"We're going to need to put on a real tourniquet," William said. I pulled a Combat Application Tourniquet (C-A-T) out of our cabinet.

A C-A-T differs from a homemade cloth tourniquet because it includes a windlass rod that can be used to achieve the necessary degree of compression. Although I'd trained with them, I'd never applied one in the field.

When I first joined our rescue squad, tourniquets were not used. Now, they're considered the standard of care. William and I applied the tourniquet. Once it was on, William removed the blood-soaked thermals.

"I'm going to take a peek." William removed the trauma dressing and irrigated the wound with sterile water. It was frighteningly deep. Once it was clean, we rebandaged it.

"How's your pain level now?" William asked.

Rory frowned. "It's still eight out of ten."

"I spoke with the ER physician. I'm going to give you something for the pain," William said. He injected pain medication into Rory's IV line.

Rory swallowed several times. He began to speak, then halted. He brushed a few strands of hair out of his eyes. "Be honest with me. Do you think I'm going to lose my leg?"

"The trauma surgeon is the only one who can answer that question, but I will say that nowadays, they are able to do incredible vessel repairs with microsurgery," William replied.

Rory nodded. "I need my leg to be able to work. If I can't work, I'll never be able to get custody of my nephews." He grew silent, lost in thought.

Once we arrived at the hospital, we were met by the trauma team. We moved Rory from our stretcher to theirs. Competent nurses and aides began caring for him while William gave his report to the trauma surgeon. I knew Rory was in great hands. I prayed they would be able to salvage his leg. It sounded like there were two young boys who were counting on him.

. . . .

A few months after the Sandy Hook Elementary School shootings in Newtown, Connecticut, in December 2012, Dr. Lenworth Jacobs

Jr., a local trauma surgeon, reviewed the victims' autopsy records. He found that many of the victims died from severe bleeding. If the bleeding could have been controlled by bystanders before EMS arrived on the scene, lives could have been saved. From these findings, the Stop the Bleed campaign was created.

The Stop the Bleed campaign includes a brief course that teaches people in the community how to help those who are suffering from bleeding emergencies. Bleeding injuries are not just limited to mass shootings. They can happen in everyday life, including in your home, in a car accident, or on the athletic fields.

I'm a certified Stop the Bleed instructor. I highly recommend this course for schools, churches, and other community clubs and groups. Even if you are afraid of blood, you can benefit from the knowledge of how to instruct others in what to do. You never know—you may even need to save your own life one day.

A few weeks after Rory's accident, we learned that he had successfully undergone surgery. His coworker's fast actions helped prevent Rory from going into shock and possibly dying. I prayed things would work out for Rory and that he'd gain custody of his nephews.

8

The Tuck In

*Even though I walk
through the darkest valley,
I will fear no evil,
for you are with me;
your rod and your staff,
they comfort me.*

PSALM 23:4

The new year was off to a busy start for our rescue squad. Our first patient was an elderly man with stomach pain and a hacking cough. I hung back and didn't get too involved in the call because I felt as though I might be coming down with a cold myself.

Our next call came close to noon. A woman in her eighties reported difficulty walking for two days. She said she'd managed to hobble around her house by using a straight cane. When she'd woken up that morning, she'd discovered she couldn't walk at all, even with a rolling walker.

While we were assisting her, we received another call for a woman across town with numbness in her left hand. A different crew handled that call.

After dinner, I decided to nurse my cold and relax. But when my pager went off, I figured I could take it easy later.

DISPATCHER: "Request for first aid at Pine Cove Apartments, building 2, apartment C, for a 39-year-old woman bleeding from the mouth."

Jose Sanchez was sitting in the driver's seat of the ambulance, and Ted O'Malley was in the front passenger seat, when I arrived at the squad building. When I climbed into the back, I found Meg Potter gathering some of the equipment we might need. We buckled up as Jose called our rig in service.

When we arrived, Jose stayed with the ambulance while the rest of us cut across a small courtyard toward building 2. Normally, the area boasts lush green grass with flower-lined sidewalks. Now, the grass was covered with a thin layer of old snow that crunched under my boots.

The apartment complex includes sturdy red-brick buildings with small balconies on the upstairs apartments and patios for the downstairs ones. Ted rang the doorbell for apartment C.

Officer Jack Endicott immediately pulled open the door and greeted us. "We've got a 39-year-old female by the name of Ria Goldstone who had dental surgery two days ago. She's worried because her mouth won't stop bleeding, and she feels like it's making her choke. She'd like to go to the hospital."

We found Ria sitting on her sofa. She'd already packed a small overnight bag, anticipating that she might be admitted to the hospital. She stood up when we entered the room, but then sat back down again. "Pardon me, but I've got a wad of gauze in my mouth to stop the bleeding, so it's hard to talk."

Ted introduced us. Meg checked Ria's vital signs, which were all normal. All things considered, it was a routine call. I wrote up the call sheet, and we helped Ria onto our stretcher. Jose, Meg, and Ted took her to Bakersville Hospital. I stayed back in case we had another call—and to make a second attempt at getting some rest before going back to work the next day.

. . . .

Eleven months later

Even as I raked our front lawn, more yellow and brown leaves floated down. Before I could finish, my pager went off.

> **DISPATCHER:** "Request for first aid at 705 Horizon Avenue for a 72-year-old female with difficulty breathing."

I tossed the rake on the ground and rushed to our first aid building. I arrived at the same time as Jose Sanchez and Jessie Barnes.

"On my portable radio I heard Dispatcher Franklin tell the patrols on scene that the paramedics have a ten-minute ETA," Jessie said. "He asked them to expedite. It sounds serious."

Within a few minutes, we pulled up in front of a small, dark-blue Cape Cod–style house. I grabbed our first aid bag, and Jessie brought the defibrillator and call sheets. A concerned woman who appeared to be in her late sixties met us at the front door. "Hi, I'm June. Please, come this way. My sister, Francesca DeWitt, needs help. She's visiting from Tennessee. We dined at a friend's house last night. Everything was fine until about 2:00 a.m. My sister woke up throwing up. At the time, I thought she had food poisoning. But now, she's complaining of having difficulty breathing."

We followed the woman upstairs to a small bedroom in the rear of the house. Francesca, who looked remarkably like her sister, was perched on the edge of the bed. The smell of stale vomit hung in the air. I began breathing through my mouth instead of my nose to avoid the odor.

Sergeant Derrick Flint had already placed Francesca on high-flow oxygen. "I have it cranked up to fifteen, but so far, it isn't helping."

Francesca tried to tug off the mask. "I can't breathe." Sweat trickled down her forehead from the effort of breathing.

I placed a blood pressure cuff around Francesca's arm and pumped it up. "Her blood pressure is difficult to hear, but it's 144 over 90. I can't feel a radial pulse. Her respiratory rate is 28, and her lung sounds are very diminished." A normal breathing rate is between 12 and 20. It was clear that Francesca was in severe respiratory distress. I noticed she wore a small gold crucifix around her neck. She gave it a quick squeeze, which I assumed was a silent plea for help from above.

"On a scale of zero to ten, if ten is the worst difficulty breathing and zero is none at all, how would you rate your difficulty breathing?" I asked.

"Nine," Francesca said. She wasn't able to speak much—another sign of her struggle to breathe.

I turned to June. "What kind of medical history does Francesca have? Does she have any allergies to medications?"

"She has high blood pressure and increased cholesterol. She doesn't have any allergies. Here's a list of her medications." June passed me an index card.

Jose and Jessie helped Francesca move from the bed to our stair chair, while I tucked the portable tank into a slot underneath the chair. Just then, paramedics Ty Fleming and Paula Pritchard arrived.

"We're going to give you a breathing treatment," Paula said. A breathing treatment, also known as a nebulizer treatment, allows medication to be administered quickly and directly into the lungs. She poured liquid medicine into a small cup and attached it to the bottom of an oxygen mask. She passed me the attached oxygen tubing, and I attached it to one of our portable oxygen tanks while Paula switched June from the non-rebreather mask to the one with the medication. "You can set the flow to eight liters per minute."

I prayed it would give Francesca quick relief.

Using the stair chair, we lifted Francesca downstairs and carried her out to the ambulance. Usually, one medic rides in the back with us, and the other drives their rig behind us to the hospital. If a person is in severe distress, both medics will stay in the back of our ambulance, and one of our crew members will drive theirs. This was one of those cases. Jose offered to drive the paramedics' ambulance, and I climbed into the back of ours with Ty and Paula.

After a minute, Francesca smiled tentatively. "It's getting easier to breathe."

I patted her arm. "That's good. We'll be at the hospital in about ten minutes."

Ty started an intravenous line, while Paula applied the 12-lead ECG. "It's a sinus rhythm but tachy," she said, meaning the rhythm was normal but rapid.

When we left Francesca at the hospital, I knew her medical situation was uncertain. She'd need testing to figure out the cause of her sudden respiratory distress.

Five hours later

> **DISPATCHER:** "Request for first aid at Pine Cove Apartments, building 2, apartment C, for a 39-year-old woman with difficulty breathing."

I recognized the address immediately. It was Ria Goldstone, the woman we'd helped earlier in the year with bleeding after dental surgery. I wondered what could be causing her respiratory distress.

Jose, Jessie, and I answered the call. Ria recognized me right away. "You're the girl who came when I was bleeding. Last week, I got diagnosed with mitral valve prolapse. Now, my left arm is going numb. I'm not sure if it's coming from my heart, or if I have a neck problem." Just like last time, Ria had her overnight bag packed and ready to go.

Paramedics Ty and Paula were already on the scene. "Ria doesn't have any difficulty breathing now, and her ECG looks normal. We're going to release her to BLS." The paramedics, who provide advanced life support, release to BLS (basic life support) in cases in which advanced care is not needed.

As we were preparing to leave, another call came.

> **DISPATCHER:** "Request for first aid on Highway 65 by the Pine Cove Convenience Store for a report of a motor vehicle accident with a patient with a head injury."

Jose and Jessie took Ria to the hospital and dropped me off at the site of the motor vehicle accident, where I met up with Ted O'Malley. Our patient was a 21-year-old female who reported that the other car had blown a red light. Although our patient had been wearing her seat belt, she said her head had struck the driver's side window.

After we assessed her, we put a cervical collar on her, placed her on a backboard, and transported her to Bakersville Hospital.

One hour later

Our first aid crew returned to the hospital with a middle-aged woman who had fallen and dislocated her shoulder. While there, I ran into Francesca DeWitt's sister in the ED hallway.

"After she was in the emergency room for a while, she began to have trouble breathing again," June told me. "They're running more tests, and then she's being admitted to the intensive care unit."

My heart went out to Francesca and her family. I had known her situation was grim, but it was even worse than I'd thought. Though she was far away from her home state of Tennessee, I was glad she had her sister to love her, pray for her, support her. To tuck her in.

. . . .

Nine days later

> **DISPATCHER:** "Request for first aid at Pine Cove Apartments, building 2, apartment C, for a 39-year-old woman with heart palpitations."

"Isn't this the same apartment we were at about a week ago?" Jose asked.

I nodded. "Yes, she was concerned about mitral valve prolapse and the numbness in her arm."

We found Ria Goldstone in her living room with Officer Brad Sims. She was sipping a glass of ginger ale. "I felt like my heart was racing earlier, but it seems to be okay now. I got scared and didn't want to be alone, so I called 911."

I checked Ria's vital signs. Everything appeared fine, though her heart rate was 96, which is at the high end of the normal range.

Ria smoothed back her hair and twisted a strand of it around her index finger. "I think maybe I was just anxious. My mom hasn't been that well lately, and I'm worried about her."

"It's understandable. Your heart rate is okay now," I said.

"I feel silly calling you, but I'm glad you came. I feel more at ease now, knowing that I'm okay. I don't want to go to the hospital."

I remembered Ria's medical history and jotted it down on our patient care form. She signed our refusal form, and we said goodbye.

Seeing Ria reminded me of the last time we were with her, which was the same day we had taken Francesca DeWitt to the hospital. Jessie had learned the previous day from her sister June that she was slowly improving. She'd been diagnosed with pneumonia as well as congestive heart failure. She was out of the intensive care unit, and they hoped she'd be discharged within a few days.

. . . .

Two months later

> **DISPATCHER:** "Request for first aid at 87 Clementine Road for a 77-year-old female with difficulty breathing."

I had just returned home from work and was about to start making spaghetti when I heard the call. I turned off the stovetop and hustled to our first aid building, where I met up with Jessie, Ted, and Meg.

When we arrived at the house on Clementine Road, we discovered an elderly woman with gray, wavy hair seated at her oak kitchen table. Although it was nearly dinner time, I noticed she had a bowl of breakfast cereal in front of her. It looked mushy, like it had been sitting there for a little while. Paramedics Ty and Paula were already assessing her.

"Mrs. Goldstone appears to be having a COPD exacerbation. We just started a nebulizer treatment," Ty said. COPD stands for chronic obstructive pulmonary disease, a chronic inflammatory lung disease that leads to obstructed airflow in the lungs. It can lead to coughing, wheezing, difficulty breathing, and increased mucus production.

After the medics finished assessing Mrs. Goldstone, we began our trip to the hospital. "I'm feeling better now," she said.

We began to chitchat. "I worry about my daughter. You nice people have taken her to the hospital several times," Mrs. Goldstone said.

"I'm sorry to hear that. Does she live with you?" I asked.

"No, she lives at Pine Cove Apartments. She had a problem with her heart valve and her heart racing. She has anxiety too."

"Is her name Ria by any chance?" I asked.

A smile brightened Mrs. Goldstone's face. "Yes, do you know her?"

I smoothed the blanket around Mrs. Goldstone's shoulders. "Yes, I've met her a couple times. I hope she's feeling better."

Mrs. Goldstone clasped my hand. "A mother always worries about her children. Thank you."

. . . .

Nine months later

> **DISPATCHER:** "Request for first aid at 87 Clementine Road for a woman with an anxiety attack."

The last rays of evening sunshine faded away as night fell. Our crew met Officer Endicott at the front door. "She's in the kitchen," he told us.

When I entered the kitchen, I expected to find Mrs. Goldstone. Instead, I found her daughter Ria.

"Oh, hi," she said. "You're probably wondering where my mother is. She passed away a few months ago. I inherited her house, so I'm in the process of moving in."

"I'm so sorry to hear that," I replied. My mind wandered back to my conversation with her mother, in which she'd said she worried about Ria. Now, her daughter was on her own.

Ria took a sip of water. "It's been a rough couple of months. I went for a walk a half hour ago, and my heart started racing. I took a Xanax, but I still don't feel great."

I checked Ria's blood pressure, pulse, and respiratory rate. "Everything is normal."

"I don't want to go to the hospital. But could you please do me a favor?"

"Sure," I replied.

"I tried to call some of my friends, but they aren't home. Do you think you could stay until I go to the bathroom? I want to go to bed, but I don't want to be alone yet."

"Of course," I said. One nice thing about volunteering with EMS in a small town is that we get to know everyone. We're a tight-knit community, and our crew is here to support people in their time of need in any way we can.

"When I didn't feel well, my mom used to get me a ginger ale from the fridge," Ria said as we walked toward the staircase to the second floor.

Officer Endicott must have overheard her. I saw him head toward the refrigerator. Our men in blue have hearts of gold. As I waited in the hallway outside the bathroom, he came up the stairs and handed me a glass of ginger ale. I stepped into Ria's bedroom, placed it on the nightstand, and turned down her covers.

A few minutes later, Ria climbed into bed. I tucked her in, turned off the light, and bid her goodnight. I think her mother, watching from heaven above, would have approved.

9

Saying Goodbye

*Hannah was praying in her heart, and her lips
were moving but her voice was not heard.*

1 SAMUEL 1:13

DISPATCHER: "Request for first aid at 1004 Wesley Avenue for a
74-year-old fall victim with a left shoulder injury."

I was just finishing a grilled cheese sandwich when my pager went off.
It crossed my mind that perhaps I shouldn't go. My neck ached from
being involved in a fender bender the previous evening. Another driver
had blown a stop sign and turned left, striking the front of my car.

I decided to shrug off my soreness and answer the call. I crammed
the last bite of sandwich into my mouth and hurried from my air-
conditioned house into the steamy outdoors.

I recognized the address. I'd been to the home twice last year for
a nice older gentleman named Al Wagner. One instance, he had felt
faint and shaky. The other time, he'd had a diabetic emergency (low
blood sugar). On both occasions, we'd found Al sitting in a padded
wicker chair in a sunroom that overlooked a pretty garden. Each time,
I'd interviewed his wife, Jean, about his past medical history, medications, and the events that had led up to the call. I was struck by how

kind and sweet she was. They had been married for just over 50 years, and I couldn't help but think they made an adorable couple.

I knew Al wasn't steady on his feet, so I thought perhaps this time he had lost his balance and took a spill. Or maybe he had become dizzy and fallen as a result.

I was almost at our first aid building when my pager went off a second time.

> **DISPATCHER:** "Re-dispatch for 1004 Wesley Avenue for a fall victim with a left shoulder injury. Patient was unconscious, now conscious, and is complaining of chest pain and difficulty breathing."

I met Greg Turner and Colleen Harper at the first aid building. Colleen, a speech-language pathologist, mentored me when I first joined the rescue squad. "It sounds like it's turning into more than just a simple fall," she said.

Greg pulled open the driver's side front door. "It sure does. I'll drive."

"Sounds good," Colleen replied. She climbed in next to him, and I stepped into the back of the rig and began donning a pair of gloves.

We parked in front of a small gray ranch house. Officer Brad Sims waved us over to the side yard. Much to my surprise, it wasn't Mr. Wagner on the ground. His wife, Jean, was lying on her back underneath a sycamore tree. "I'm so glad it's you," she said as soon as she spotted me. All thoughts of my sore neck muscles disappeared, and I was glad I'd come.

"I'm sorry it's under these circumstances. What happened?" I asked.

"I came out to water my begonias. I began to feel dizzy, and everything started getting dark. The next thing I knew, I was on the ground. Then my chest started hurting, and I couldn't catch my breath. Fortunately, Al was sitting in the sunroom and saw me go down. He called 911 right away."

"How are you feeling now? Is the chest pain getting better or worse?" I asked her how she would rate her pain on a scale of zero to ten.

Jean frowned. "The pain is getting worse, I'm afraid. It's a ten out of ten."

I placed a blood pressure cuff around Jean's right upper arm. "Is the pain radiating anywhere or staying in the same spot?"

Jean pointed to the center of her chest. "It's staying right here. I've never had chest pain before."

Jean had a past medical history of high blood pressure and increased cholesterol. Greg wrote up the patient call sheet while Colleen slipped a sling around Jean's left shoulder. Meanwhile, I finished taking her vital signs. "Her blood pressure is 156 over 90, and her pulse is 108. Her pulse ox is 98 percent on high-flow oxygen, and her respiratory rate is 20." Jean was pushing the upper limit of a normal respiratory rate. Her blood pressure and pulse were both high. Although her pulse ox reading was normal, it may have been because she was receiving oxygen. Because she was experiencing chest pain, I followed our protocol and gave her an aspirin to chew.

Paramedics Arthur Williamson and Kennisha Smythe arrived just as we loaded Jean into our ambulance. They used their advanced training to perform a 12-lead ECG, start an intravenous line, and administer medications such as nitroglycerin.

I sat in the small side seat of the rig on the way to the hospital. Jean held my hand tightly. "I hope Al will be okay at home by himself. I haven't been in the hospital since my children were born."

"Do your children live in town?" I asked.

Jean readjusted the position of her oxygen mask. "My daughter Gigi does."

"Then I'm sure she'll watch out for Al. You just concentrate on getting better."

Jean nodded. "God bless all of you for helping me. I really appreciate it."

We brought Jean into the ED, and Kennisha gave her report to the triage nurse. After we moved Jean from our stretcher to the hospital's, we said goodbye.

We later learned that Jean suffered a heart attack that day. After undergoing open-heart surgery, she made a full recovery.

. . . .

Two years later

> **DISPATCHER:** "Request for first aid at 1004 Wesley Avenue for a 76-year-old with a possible stroke."

Jessie Barnes, Archie Harris, and I responded to the first aid call. We found Jean sitting on the couch in her living room. A middle-aged woman stood next to her.

"Hello. Do you remember me?" Jean asked.

I noticed her words were slightly slurred. "Yes, of course," I replied.

Jean pointed to a small table covered with family photos. "My husband passed away since I last saw you."

"I'm so sorry to hear that. He was such a nice man. What's going on today that made you call 911?" I asked.

"Well, three weeks ago I was diagnosed with a sinus infection. I finished the antibiotic treatment but didn't seem to be any better. I went back to the doctor, and he suggested I see a neurologist. I haven't had a chance to get to one yet. About two weeks ago, I started having trouble speaking." Jean squeezed the forearm of the woman standing next to her. "My daughter Gigi decided it was time for me to go to the hospital."

I was puzzled by Jean's symptoms. I thought it was an excellent decision to go to the emergency department. They could evaluate her to see if she might have had a stroke or if something else was causing her symptoms.

Archie performed the FAST assessment on Jean. FAST is a test endorsed by the American Stroke Association, which we perform in the field to determine if a person might be having a stroke. The acronym stands for "facial drooping," "arm weakness," "speech difficulty," and "time to call 911."

First, we assess a person's face for symmetry. Is one side drooping? Is one side of the face numb? We ask the patient to smile. Is the smile asymmetrical or lopsided? Next, we ask the person to raise both arms overhead to check for weakness. Does one arm go up higher than the other? Does the person have trouble keeping one of their arms up? Is the arm numb? Then we ask the person to repeat a short, simple phrase. Are the words slurred? Is it difficult to understand what they are saying?

If the answer to any of these questions is yes, the person should be transported to the hospital for treatment.

Jean's face was symmetrical, and her arm strength was normal. However, her words remained slurred. The medics were not available, so we loaded her into our ambulance and transported her to the hospital.

Jean's forehead creased with lines of worry. "I hope they figure out what's wrong with me."

I squeezed her hand. "Me too."

. . . .

Five months later

It had been a long flight, and David Wagner was relieved to finally be dropped off by a limousine service in front of his mother's house in Pine Cove. He'd taken two weeks off from work to stay with Jean. The last months had been difficult for his mom, and David was looking forward to spending quality time with her.

After months of uncertainty, Jean was diagnosed with amyotrophic lateral sclerosis (ALS). ALS is often called Lou Gehrig's disease, named after the famous baseball player who contracted the disease in the 1930s. It is a progressive neurodegenerative neuromuscular disease resulting in the loss of motor neurons that control voluntary muscles. In other words, it's a nervous system disease that affects nerve cells in the brain and spinal column, leading to a loss of muscle control. Since the disease is progressive, the symptoms worsen over time. Although much research is being performed, there is no cure for ALS. Currently, the disease is fatal.

ALS can present in different ways. Some people may first discover an arm has grown weak. Perhaps they have trouble opening a jar. Others first notice weakness in one or both legs. Maybe they begin tripping or perceive their balance is a little "off." In Jean's case, the disease affected the muscles that control speech and swallowing. This is known as a bulbar onset.

David had lost his father the previous year. His heart tightened at the thought of losing his mother as well. He'd told her not to wait up. "Just leave the front door unlocked," he'd said. Now, he placed his luggage on the porch and pulled open the front door. He immediately spotted Jean lying unconscious on the sofa, her face blue.

"Mom!" David shouted. He shook her shoulder, but she didn't respond. He grabbed the cordless phone from its charger on the small table next to his mother and dialed 911.

"It's my mother. She's unconscious…"

· · · · · · · · · · · · ·

DISPATCHER: "Request for first aid at 1004 Wesley Avenue for an unresponsive female with a cardiac history."

I awoke with a jolt when my pager beeped just past 1:00 a.m. It wasn't my crew night, but I always keep my pager on "just in case." I realized the call must be for Jean, so I decided to respond and be an extra set of hands for the regular crew.

When I entered the home, Sergeant Derrick Flint was checking Jean's blood pressure. I was relieved to see she was now alert and conscious.

A middle-aged man stepped forward. "This is Jean Wagner. I'm her son, David. I flew in to visit Mom for the holidays. I arrived late because my flight was delayed. When I got here, I found Mom unconscious on the sofa, and her face was blue. I shook her and called her name, but she didn't respond. I called 911, and she came around after a minute or two."

"That must have been a terrible shock for you. I've met your mother before," I said.

Although Jean's face was no longer cyanotic (blue), it was markedly pale. I pinched the nose piece on the oxygen mask she was wearing so that it wouldn't slide down her face.

"My mother was diagnosed with ALS last month. It went straight to her throat. She can whisper, but it can be difficult to understand her. She just got a communication board last week," David said.

ALS. I couldn't believe it. Poor Jean. Now, it all made sense. The slurred speech wasn't a stroke after all. It was one of the first signs of her disease.

Jean reached for her communication board and pointed to several words and pictures to say she felt a little better but still didn't feel right.

Jessie, Archie, and Greg arrived with the ambulance. I stepped off to the side with the call sheet to ask David some questions.

David ran a hand through his hair. "I'm worried because Mom's having a lot of difficulty managing her secretions. I mean, she chokes on her mucus. Part of me can't believe the whole thing. It's like a nightmare. Everything's happening so fast."

"I'm so sorry both of you have to go through this," I replied. My words felt inadequate. What can you say to a person who has lost his father and now will lose his mother as well?

I jotted down Jean's date of birth, allergies, and medications. I recalled her past medical history of myocardial infarction and open-heart surgery.

We helped Jean onto our stretcher and brought her out to the ambulance. Since it wasn't my crew night, I didn't ride to the hospital with her. Instead, I drove home with a heavy heart. Although there were several hours left before I had to get up for work, sleep eluded me. I prayed Jean would find comfort from her son's visit and wouldn't suffer.

. . . .

Three weeks later

My mother had made one of my favorite meals, stuffed peppers, for dinner. Just as I popped the last mouthful in, my pager went off.

DISPATCHER: "Request for first aid at 1004 Wesley Avenue for a 76-year-old choking victim."

I jumped to my feet. Time is of the essence for choking victims.

"It sounds serious," Mom said. "I hope she's all right. I'll save dessert for you."

I pulled on my winter coat. "Thanks."

I didn't live far from Jean. Rather than drive to the first aid building, I decided to go directly to her house.

Sergeant Flint arrived at the same time I did. We found Jean seated at the kitchen table. Her eyes bulged wide open in fear. She grabbed my hand and pulled it to her throat.

Jean's daughter Gigi stood next to her. "My mom's choking on mucus. It's not something you can do the Heimlich maneuver for."

Sergeant Flint slipped a pulse ox on Jean. "Fifty-four percent." Normal is 98 to 100 percent.

The situation was critical. Jean was pulling in a small amount of oxygen, but it wasn't nearly enough. My heart hammered in my chest. By now, after so many first aid calls, I considered Jean a friend. I desperately wanted to help her. "As soon as the ambulance arrives, we can suction you."

"I think the medical supply company delivered a suction unit a few days ago," Gigi said.

"That's great! Where is it?" I asked.

"It's on the dining room table," Gigi replied. Sergeant Flint and I followed her around the corner into a dark dining room. She flipped on the light switch. All I saw on the table was a cardboard box, sealed shut with packing tape. My heart sank. They had never opened the box.

I sent Gigi back to the kitchen to stay with Jean. Then I ripped open the box. The good news: Inside were all the parts to a suction unit. The bad news: The unit still had to be assembled! I am not exactly what you would call mechanically inclined. And this suction unit was different from our squad's machines. I knew I had only seconds to figure out how to put it together.

Sergeant Flint began pulling the clear protective plastic off the various parts and handing them to me. There certainly wasn't time to read an instruction manual. Using my knowledge of our suction units, I connected the parts together as quickly as possible and rushed back into the kitchen.

Most often, we suction patients during cardiopulmonary resuscitation (CPR). Rarely do we suction conscious patients. When we do, it's usually for frothy sputum. Certainly, never for a life-threatening mucus plug.

Jean grabbed the suction catheter out of my hand and shoved it down her throat. I held my finger over the small hole on the catheter to ensure it would provide suction.

After 15 seconds, Jean removed the catheter from her throat and took in deep breaths. Her oxygen-starved lungs sucked in life-saving air. *Thank You, Jesus.*

Jean must have dislodged the mucus plug because her oxygen saturation (pulse ox reading) began quickly rising. She held a high-flow oxygen mask near her face. I didn't secure the straps in case she wanted to suction herself again.

Squad members Colleen and Archie arrived with the ambulance. As we brought Jean out to the rig, paramedics Arthur and Kennisha arrived. Once they finished assessing Jean, they asked Colleen to switch her from the high-flow oxygen mask to a nasal cannula set to a rate of two liters per minute. Jean's cheeks turned rosy, and her breathing appeared normal.

On the drive, we reminisced about the calls for Mr. Wagner in their sunroom. Jean smiled, apparently lost in fond memories of her husband. She squeezed my hand tightly. A few minutes later, after we arrived at the hospital, Kennisha gave her report to the triage nurse.

Jean wrote on a piece of paper, "I feel like I'm starting to plug up again." I was relieved she was in the hospital, in competent and caring hands.

Later, when we were cleaning up our ambulance, we critiqued our response to the call. "What could we have done differently?" I asked.

"You could see if Jean has an 18-French catheter at home if it happens again. That would be easier to use and more comfortable for her than the Yankauer," Kennisha replied. A Yankauer is rigid, whereas a French catheter is thinner and more flexible.

Our conversation was interrupted by our next first aid call.

DISPATCHER: "Request for first aid at Little River Assisted Living Facility for an 89-year-old male with vertigo who is vomiting."

Kennisha stepped out of the ambulance, and our crew headed back to town to handle the emergency. The call was fairly routine. Our patient appeared to have a bad stomach bug. After we transported him to the hospital and transferred care of him to the ED staff, Archie and I slipped into Jean's room to check on her progress.

"How's it going?" Archie asked.

"She's still not feeling great," Gigi replied.

I explained what Kennisha had said about using an 18-French catheter.

"We definitely don't have that at home. I'm not sure how fast we can get one either," Gigi said.

As Archie continued to visit with them, I slipped outside to get an 18-French catheter from our ambulance. I wanted to make sure Jean had all the tools she needed in case she got plugged up again. She was discharged a few hours later.

Two days later

While working as a physical therapist in the hospital, I asked a respiratory therapist if she had any advice for our squad with regard to treating Jean. She suggested a cough assist machine for home use. It's a type of machine designed to noninvasively help clear secretions from a person's airway.

When I saw Sergeant Flint on a first aid call later that same day, I told him about the machine.

"I visited Jean yesterday," he said. "I plan to check in on her again tomorrow. I can relay the information then."

I was touched that he was looking in on her. I feel blessed to live in a small town in which everyone cares about one another. We're all part of Jesus's circle of love.

· · · · · · · · · · · · · ·

Four months later

> **DISPATCHER:** "Request for first aid at 1004 Wesley Avenue for a medical alarm activation."

I happened to be covering for Helen McGuire for the first few hours of her crew night. The call went out exactly one minute before she was scheduled to take over. As it turned out, we both answered the call.

Since Jean could no longer speak, I was glad she had a medical alert system in which she could simply press a button for help. While I was driving to our first aid building, my pager went off again.

> **DISPATCHER:** "Update for request for first aid at 1004 Wesley Avenue: Victim is a 76-year-old fall victim complaining of left hip pain."

When we arrived at Jean's home, we found her lying in her bedroom on her left side. She pointed to her left hip and wrote down on a piece of paper that it hurt. I was glad she'd landed on carpeting and not hardwood. I prayed her hip was just bruised and not fractured. She already had enough on her plate.

Archie, Helen, Jessie, and I carefully maneuvered Jean onto our scoop—a stretcher that splits into two pieces so it can be used to "scoop" a person up without rolling them. I glanced at her night table. On the corner, close to her bed, was a copy of the Bible.

As we placed Jean into the ambulance, her daughter Gigi arrived. "Mom's on hospice now. Do you think you're allowed to take her to the hospital?"

My heart sank at the news that Jean was on hospice. The disease was progressing rapidly. "Yes, a fall is a special exception," I replied.

Helen drove, and Archie sat next to her to be her copilot. Jessie and I sat in the back with Jean. I placed a cold pack on her left hip to numb the pain, then sat in the small side seat next to her stretcher. I held her hand tightly on the way to the hospital.

A lump formed in my throat. Since Jean was on hospice, I knew I probably wouldn't see her again. This was goodbye.

Although the scoop limited Jean's movement, she reached for me and pulled me close. As difficult as it was for her to speak any words, she said, "I love you."

I hugged her tightly. "I love you too."

. . . .

I think of Jean each time I drive past her street. She fought valiantly against a heartbreaking disease with faith and dignity. My friendship with Jean inspired me to specialize in ALS as a physical therapist.

Wading Through a Winter Wonderland

When the storm has swept by, the wicked are gone,
but the righteous stand firm forever.

PROVERBS 10:25

I turned on the television, eager to listen to the latest weather forecast. "A major snowstorm is working its way up the coast," the meteorologist said. "Expect eight to twelve inches of snow, along with blizzard-like conditions, which will make traveling treacherous. Winds will be in excess of fifty miles per hour. Snow will spread across the state from south to north, starting in the late afternoon."

When we have snowstorms, a crew volunteers to sleep overnight at the first aid building. That way, we don't have to worry about having a delayed response. This time, Jessie Barnes, Jose Sanchez, and I volunteered to stay at the building during the storm. Likewise, the fire department would be standing by next door at their building. In bad storms, they sometimes help us with things like shoveling the first aid victim's walkway so we can get him or her safely out to the ambulance.

The hours ticked by, and a thick blanket of snow covered our property. Jose planned to pick me up at 7:00 p.m. We don't bring our cars to the squad building because we need to leave the parking lot open for the snowplows to be able to work.

Seven o'clock came and went. I figured Jose must be running late. At eight o'clock, I turned on my police radio just in time to hear Jose say the ambulance was stuck. He requested a borough plow to come dig him out. A short while later, my phone rang.

"I hate to say it, but there's been a change in plans," Jose said. "I'm not going to be able to pick you up because the snow is already too deep."

It was one of the first times I would not be part of the "blizzard crew." I fell asleep that night hoping there wouldn't be any first aid calls.

There weren't any.

That night, that is.

When I awoke the next morning, I figured I'd grab a bite to eat, and then we could start digging out. I peered out the front door. Deep snow blanketed the earth.

I decided to peek out the back door as well. I opened the family-room curtains, revealing a patio door that opens onto our deck. To my surprise, all I could see was white. The blizzard's swirling winds must have piled snow up as high as our door.

I donned my snow pants, grabbed a yardstick, and waded through the snow on our driveway. I stuck the yardstick down into the snow in several places. It was 36 inches deep at the lowest point.

Three feet of snow! It's too high for our snowblower. With this much snow, it would probably take days for a snowplow to uncover our street.

A few hours later, as my family and I were undertaking the mammoth task of shoveling out, my pager went off.

> **DISPATCHER:** "Request for first aid at 821 Hanover Road for a 38-year-old male with severe finger lacerations from a snowblower accident."

The address was well over half a mile away. Since our road was unplowed and our driveway only partially shoveled, I couldn't drive there. *Well, I guess I'm going to miss this one.* I hate missing first aid calls.

An idea blossomed in my (frosty) head. *Maybe I can run there.* I'm out of shape now, but I used to run track when I was younger. I figured the ambulance would take longer than normal to get to the scene because it would have to battle its way through partially plowed roads.

The storm clouds were gone, but an icy wind blew puffs of swirling white. Bright sunshine dazzled on the sparkling snow. I blinked twice, regretting that I wasn't wearing sunglasses.

We had already dug a path from our front door to the road, so the first 50 feet of my journey along our driveway went quite smoothly. That ended abruptly when I reached the street. The snow came well above my waist. My vision of rushing through the snow melted like snowflakes on warm asphalt. I found myself wading through a winter wonderland.

I worked my way past the first two houses on my block, albeit slowly. Honestly, it felt more like passing 20 houses. Numerous neighbors had ventured outdoors to begin the daunting task of shoveling out. Most of them know I volunteer with the first aid squad.

"Are you going on a call?" one shouted out to me.

"Yeah," I responded. I kept my answer short, conserving my breath.

Another clapped. "You go, girl! I hope you don't have to go too far."

My lungs burned from the effort of pushing my legs through the snow. My arms were swinging like they usually do when I run. However, my lower half felt like it was slowly grinding through mud. In my eagerness to move quickly, my upper body lunged forward faster than the rest of me. I lost my balance and threw my hands out. They sank deeply into the snow in front of me. I would have fallen completely, except my legs were firmly rooted in snow. I glanced to the left and right. My cheeks turned pink. *I hope no one saw that.* Icy snow slid down the inside of my gloves and along my forearms.

When I turned left onto the next street, I was relieved to find a single lane had been roughly plowed. It still had about a foot of snow on it, but it was certainly much better than three feet. I began jogging in the tire tracks and prayed no cars would venture down the road.

By the time I arrived at the scene, I thought I might need first aid myself. (Just kidding—but I did pause a few yards away to try to discreetly catch my breath.) To my surprise, I had beaten our ambulance. Two police officers, Jack Endicott and Brad Sims, stood next to a gentleman with short brown hair wearing a royal-blue ski jacket. Officer

Endicott was supporting the man's right arm, and Officer Sims was applying a bulky dressing to his hand.

When Officer Endicott spotted me, he said, "This is Cal Thornton. He's definitely going to need stitches on his fingertips."

Cal grimaced. "I did something I really regret."

I could guess without Cal going into detail. We get a snowblower call every year or two. The snowblower gets clogged with icy snow or other debris and stops running. The person sticks their hand in to clear out whatever is causing the jam. Unfortunately, once the person is successful, the snowblower immediately kicks into gear again. The blades contact the person's hand. You get the picture. It usually isn't pretty.

I glanced down the road and saw our rig slogging its way closer. A fire truck pulled up to see if we needed assistance.

Jessie Barnes stepped out of the ambulance, along with Helen McGuire, Jose Sanchez, and Sadie Martinez. Sadie, a competent dental hygienist with a quick wit, is a talented EMT and fun to be around.

"We can walk him to the ambulance and fill out the paperwork in there," I said.

Jessie nodded. "I'm going to check with police headquarters about the best route to the hospital. It was really tough getting here, and I'm not sure if there are road closures."

"There are probably a lot of roads that haven't been fully plowed yet," Helen agreed.

Sadie and I helped Cal step into the side entrance of our rig and got him settled into the stretcher. I pulled the seat-belt straps tight and fastened them securely.

"Jose and I will stay back in case there's another call," Helen said. "I think you should bring one of the firemen with you in case you get stuck. I'll ask Brandon Shapiro." Brandon was a good choice. He was young and strong. Plus, he was holding a snow shovel.

"Great idea," I agreed. As a crew member who has helped dig our ambulance out of both snow and sand, I can tell you firsthand it's not easy. One night a few years ago, our ambulance got stuck trying to pick me up for a snowstorm standby. Neighbors from nearly every house on my street ventured out to assist us. It was one of those magical moments in which people drop whatever they are doing to help.

I buckled myself into the small side seat next to Cal. Sadie sat on the bench across from me. Brandon climbed in and sat in the captain's chair, which is located in front of the stretcher, close to the cab.

"Thanks so much for riding with us," I said to Brandon.

"No problem. All I was doing was shoveling snow," he replied.

Shoveling snow was probably what we'd all be doing for days to come. I glanced at my watch. It usually takes us 13 minutes to get to the hospital from this area. It would easily take us double that. After that, I needed to rejoin my family for some serious shoveling.

"The dispatcher isn't aware of any road closures. I'm going to try to take Highway 13," Jessie called back to us.

Highway 13 is our normal route to the hospital. I didn't envy Jessie the task of driving. I began filling out Cal's call sheet, and Sadie took his vital signs. Some blood began soaking through his dressing, so we applied another layer of bandages.

"How's your pain level?" Sadie asked.

"Bad," Cal admitted.

I pulled a cold pack out of the cabinet next to me and placed it over the dressing. "Once we get to the ED, the doctor will be able to give you pain medication."

"How far away is the hospital?" he asked.

Sadie glanced out the window to see where we were. "We're almost at the Marina Beach Bridge, so normally it would be another ten minutes. Today, it may take another twenty."

The Marina Beach Bridge is a large bridge connecting Marina Beach with the next town. I hoped they had done a good job sanding the bridge, because we'd need good traction on the way down.

As we got closer to the bridge, the ambulance slid to a stop. "We've got a problem," Jessie told us. "The bridge hasn't even been plowed yet. There's no way we'll get over it."

"How about the Throckmorton Bridge?" I asked. That bridge was much smaller. It was just a few blocks east of our current location.

"Let me check with dispatch," Jessie replied.

I gazed out the window behind us. A few brave souls had ventured out onto the roads. Since the bridge was closed, some of them were trying to turn around. Several were stuck, tires spinning fruitlessly.

"The dispatcher thinks Throckmorton Bridge is open. We'll head that way," Jessie said. But as he tried to get the rig moving again, the wheels began spinning. Now, we were stuck too.

"That's why you brought me," Brandon said. He grabbed his shovel and hopped out.

"I wish we had another shovel," Sadie said.

"Me too." Our area had never experienced a blizzard of this magnitude in my lifetime. Our ambulance had never become stuck in snow on the way to the hospital.

Sadie rooted around in one of the cabinets and pulled out a pink emesis (vomit) basin. We exchanged a look, trying not to giggle. "Well, here's my shovel. You stay with Cal, and I'll help Brandon."

I wondered if this could be the first time in history that a flimsy emesis basin doubled as a snow shovel. I glanced out the window and watched as Sadie fervently tried to shovel snow from near the ambulance's tires. As you can imagine, the basin didn't hold much snow. I wished I could snap a photo to capture the moment.

A few minutes later, the two climbed back in. "That should do it," Brandon said. The ambulance crawled through a few local roads to the next bridge. Much to our dismay, it also hadn't been plowed.

Jessie called dispatch again. "How about the bridge by the ocean?"

"That one's definitely closed," the dispatcher replied.

We paused, uncertain which way to go next. I could tell Cal was in significant pain. Time ticked by. We needed to get him to Bakersville Hospital to be stitched up.

"We'll have to backtrack. We could maybe take Route 4," Jessie said.

Route 4 is a large highway. There are no businesses or houses along it. If we slid off the road there, it would be too far to walk for help. It was difficult to imagine how we'd be able to negotiate the entrance and exit ramps.

"Never mind," Jessie said after a moment. "Route 4 is closed."

I had an idea. "I'll text Helen. I think she's friends with a plastic surgeon." I fired off a text to her. If the surgeon had supplies in his home, perhaps he could stitch up Cal's wounds.

I'll give it a try and let you know, Helen replied.

"The only other way would be back roads, but if these highways aren't even plowed yet, I can't imagine getting through those," Jessie said.

At this point, an hour and a half had passed since we began our trip. I was beginning to realize that we might never get to Bakersville Hospital. I was relieved this patient wasn't in critical condition.

Sorry. Bad news, Helen texted. *He said he would have sewn him up in his home, but he's away in Florida right now.*

Another avenue blocked, this time figuratively rather than literally.

"I can't tell you how sorry I am to put you through all this," Cal said. "I know you're volunteers."

"Don't worry about that. We don't mind," Sadie replied.

"I think our only option at this point is to try to get to Harrison Hospital," Jessie said. Harrison was much farther away than Bakersville. It would also involve going over a large bridge. All we could do was try. And pray.

Another hour passed. The ambulance crawled closer to Harrison Hospital.

How's it going? Helen texted.

We just made it over the bridge, I replied.

Hope blossomed. The roads ahead looked clear enough to get through. It wouldn't be easy, but it looked like we were going to make it.

Thirty minutes later, we delivered Cal into the hands of the Harrison Hospital staff. Finally, he would receive the medical care he needed. To date, we've never again had to use an emesis basin as a snow shovel.

11

Dance Till You Drop

It is by grace you have been saved, through faith—
and this is not from yourselves, it is the gift of God.

EPHESIANS 2:8-9

I hummed along with my car radio as I coasted down the Marina Beach Bridge on the way home from work. My last physical therapy patient had canceled their appointment, so I took an hour of vacation time and started my weekend early. Mentally, I filled my "found hour" with a list of possible activities, such as stopping by the post office, starting a load of laundry, and taking my miniature dachshund, Schnitzel, for a walk.

My plans changed when my pager went off.

DISPATCHER: *"Request for first aid at the intersection of Kensington Avenue and Winding Brook Road for a pedestrian struck by a motor vehicle. Patient is currently unconscious with injuries."*

The call was for an incident only a mile away from my current location. I headed toward the scene, figuring I could meet our ambulance there.

Sergeant Derrick Flint's police car was parked at the nearest intersection in a way that blocked traffic from entering. I squeezed around it and parked close to the scene of the accident. After slipping on a pair of medical gloves, I grabbed my first aid kit and went to see how I could help.

A dark-blue sedan was parked in the middle of the road. Officer Jack Endicott led a middle-aged gentleman from the car to the side of the road and helped him sit down on the curb.

An older-looking woman lay on her back in the road, close to a parked gray coupe. Sergeant Flint was holding stabilization on her head and neck. "This is Georgette Purchase," he told me. "We're not sure yet if she was getting into or out of her car when she was struck. She was unconscious when I arrived, but she's starting to come around now."

Georgette moaned in pain. Her right lower leg was deformed, indicating a probable fracture.

"She has a laceration on the back of her head," Sergeant Flint said.

"Do you want me to take over stabilization so you can do the accident investigation?" I asked.

"That would be great," he said. We switched positions, and he began determining exactly what had transpired to land Georgette in this position.

"My leg," Georgette whimpered. "What happened?"

I placed my hands on either side of her head to stabilize her cervical spine. "You were hit by a car. I want you to stay very still and try not to move your head. Does anything hurt besides your leg?"

"My shoulder hurts. And my back hurts. What happened?"

Just then, Jessie Barnes, Helen McGuire, Archie Harris, and Jose Sanchez arrived with two ambulances. Helen began performing a head-to-toe assessment of Georgette, while Archie worked on getting a set of vital signs. Jose went to check on the status of the driver of the other car.

Helen systematically examined Georgette from the top of her head to her feet. "We'll need to bandage the back of her head. The right lower leg is deformed, so we'll need to splint it. Her right shoulder and lower back are tender to the touch. We'll need a collar and backboard." Jessie went to gather the necessary equipment from our ambulance.

Archie pulled the stethoscope from his ears. "Her blood pressure is 140 over 92, and her heart rate is 98 and regular."

Georgette pushed his hand away. "I want to go home."

"We're going to take you to the hospital so a doctor can check you out," Helen explained as she began bandaging Georgette's head.

Georgette's eyes opened wide with surprise. "Why?"

"You've been in an accident. Do you remember what happened?" Helen asked.

Georgette scrunched her brows. "Really? An accident? No, I didn't know that."

After Helen bandaged Georgette's head, she placed a cervical collar around her neck. Sergeant Flint came over to update us. "We've been talking to Georgette's neighbors and a witness. Georgette was entering her car when she was struck. She was most likely going to volunteer at the food bank, which she always does on Wednesday afternoons. The man who struck her claims he passed out."

I glanced over at the driver of the car that had struck Georgette. He way lying on the grass, holding his head. Jose knelt next to him, checking his vital signs.

"There are no skid marks," Sergeant Flint said. "Based on the witness's observations, we're guessing the car that struck her was traveling at thirty-five miles per hour."

That's fast enough to cause significant injuries. I hoped she didn't have any life-threatening damage to her internal organs. Archie and I applied a splint to Georgette's right leg while Jessie prepped a backboard. We'd need to immobilize Georgette with the backboard in case she had suffered a spinal cord injury.

Georgette blinked. "What's going on?"

Repetitive questioning is a classic sign of a concussion. Georgette knew her name but was confused as to the current month and year. In addition, she was amnesic regarding the events leading up to the accident. Given that she had lost consciousness, she had a concussion at minimum. Hopefully, she didn't have any bleeding in her brain.

"What medical problems do you have?" Helen asked.

"Let me think for a minute. Let's see… I have high blood pressure and high cholesterol," Georgette replied.

Helen slid the backboard alongside Georgette. "Do you know the names of your medications?"

"I don't like doctors and hospitals. I don't take any medications. I want to go home," Georgette responded.

"First, we're going to take you to the hospital to make sure you are okay," Helen said. As a unit, we rolled Georgette onto her side, then we carefully log-rolled her back onto the backboard.

Once we placed her in the ambulance, paramedics Ty Fleming and Paula Pritchard arrived and began their assessment. Helen climbed into the driver's seat, and Jessie and I hopped into the back. "Jose and Archie are going to take the driver of the car to the hospital. He's still complaining of dizziness," Helen said.

I reflected on how I was glad I happened to get out of work early that day to lend a hand. I hoped both patients would be okay.

. . . .

Later that day, after the warm autumn rays of sunshine had given way to chilly darkness, my pager went off again.

> **DISPATCHER:** "Request for first aid at Ocean Spray Manor for an 82-year-old male who's unresponsive and not breathing. Possible CPR in progress."

Helen and I missed the ambulance by a hair, so we followed it to the scene. We parked behind it in the yellow zone, close to the entrance of the restaurant. All the regular parking spaces were already taken. I figured some kind of event was going on.

A backboard was leaning against the rear right corner of the ambulance. I grabbed it on my way by and carried it into the dining room.

A large group of people had formed a circle around an unconscious elderly man who lay spread-eagle on the carpet, close to the dance floor.

Helen and I worked our way through the crowd to the victim. His face was pale, with a bluish tinge around his lips.

Jessie Barnes, Archie Harris, and Kerry Branson were kneeling next to the patient. Kerry, an accomplished architect, enjoys spending time volunteering with the rescue squad to serve her community. She measured the patient for an oropharyngeal (oral) airway and inserted it into his mouth. An oral airway helps to keep an unconscious person's airway open by preventing the tongue from covering the epiglottis.

A man I didn't recognize knelt at the patient's head and was providing rescue breathing with a bag valve mask. Defibrillator pads were on the victim's chest. Jessie was performing chest compressions.

Officer Endicott handed me our patient clipboard to fill out. "I'm going to move this crowd into the hallway to give you room to work. What I know so far is that Henry Burger collapsed, and bystanders started CPR. The man doing the rescue breathing is a physician. He shocked Henry twice so far with the restaurant's defibrillator, but Henry hasn't regained a pulse." He pointed to a birdlike elderly woman sitting at a nearby table. "That's Henry's wife."

I slipped into the seat next to Mrs. Burger. "Excuse me. My name is Andrea, and I'm a member of the first aid squad. Is it okay if I ask you a few questions?"

Mrs. Burger pushed her eyeglasses farther up the bridge of her nose and turned her attention to me. "Yes, of course. What would you like to know?"

I poised my pen above the patient run report. "Can you tell me what happened tonight?"

"This is our friend's son's wedding. My husband, Henry, is overweight and hasn't done a bit of exercise in many years. So far tonight, he's drunk four glasses of wine. A little while ago, he got up and danced like crazy for ten minutes. Then he plopped down next to me and began eating pasta." Mrs. Burger's eyes filled with tears.

I patted her hand. "What happened after that?"

"Well, he said he was having a hard time swallowing the pasta, but eventually he got it down. The next thing I knew, he collapsed right on top of me."

I couldn't help but think what a horrible shock it must have been for her. After filling out Henry's address and date of birth, I asked, "Does he have any medical problems?"

"He used to have high blood pressure, but now it's under control with medications. He had a hernia repair last year. I don't remember what medications he takes, but he probably has a list of them in his wallet."

Mrs. Burger leaned forward and looked at her husband. Jessie was just about to press the button on the defibrillator to deliver a third shock. "Is Henry dead?"

When Mrs. Burger asked me the question, Henry was indeed clinically dead. He didn't have a pulse, and he wasn't breathing. Precious seconds were ticking by.

Mrs. Burger placed her hand on my forearm. "What I mean is, how long can you keep doing what you're doing before it's no use anymore?"

I didn't answer her question directly. Instead, I said, "We're breathing for him right now. Soon, the paramedics will be here from the hospital and will give him medications for his heart."

Mrs. Burger frowned. "I wish he took better care of himself."

I noticed that no shock was advised from the defibrillator, which was not a good sign. I excused myself from Mrs. Burger and crouched near her husband's head. "How can I help?" I asked.

Jessie glanced up at me. "You can suction him."

"Got it." Fluid was leaking from the corner of Mr. Burger's mouth. The doctor paused from delivering ventilations long enough for me to insert the suction catheter. Using a figure-eight technique, I sucked out the liquid.

"I'm going to try to shock again. Everyone clear," Jessie said, raising his arm up and over Mr. Burger's body to make sure none of us were touching him. This time, when Jessie pressed the analyze button on the defibrillator, it began revving up to deliver a shock. I held my breath as Jessie pressed the button. Joules of potentially life-saving energy coursed through Mr. Burger's chest. I offered up a quick, silent prayer it would work.

Jessie palpated Henry's carotid artery. "I feel a strong pulse."

The doctor felt the other side of Henry's neck. "I feel it too. Hold chest compressions." He resumed providing ventilations to Mr. Burger.

Kerry pressed her index and middle fingers into the thumb-side of Henry's wrist. "I've got a strong radial pulse now too."

My heart filled with hope.

More fluid bubbled up from Henry's mouth. Coordinating with the doctor, I suctioned again.

"Time to get him on a backboard," Helen said as she slid one alongside Henry.

As we rolled him onto it and began fastening the straps, paramedics Ty and Paula arrived. After Helen briefed them, Paula placed electrodes on Henry's chest, arms, and legs so she could analyze his heart rhythm with a 12-lead ECG. "He's having an acute MI," she said. In other words, he was having a heart attack (myocardial infarction).

Henry began vomiting. We rolled him, backboard and all, onto his side. Jessie suctioned him, and then we returned him to a supine position.

Ty went to Henry's wife and began speaking to her in hushed tones. "His situation is extremely critical," I overheard him say. Although Henry had regained his pulse, he was unresponsive and not breathing. His condition remained unstable.

Helen clipped together the backboard strap near Henry's calves. "Hey, he's starting to move his legs."

I looked first at Henry's legs and then at his face. I thought I saw his eyes flicker open for a second, but the movement was so brief I couldn't be sure.

"Let's get him in the rig," Paula said.

Just then, rousing cheers and applause broke out in the hallway. The wedding guests must have gotten word that Henry had his pulse back. However, it was still an uphill battle. He needed to start breathing on his own again.

We lifted Henry onto our stretcher. This time, I was certain he briefly opened his eyes. *Maybe he's starting to wake up.*

Archie and Kerry wheeled the stretcher out to the ambulance. Jessie walked alongside them, continuing to provide rescue breaths to

Henry. When we reached the ambulance, Kerry climbed into the driver's seat, and Jessie, Archie, and I climbed into the back with Paula. Helen stayed back in case we had another first aid call in town. Soon, we were on our way.

I wish I could tell you it was a smooth, uneventful ride to the hospital. But it wasn't. After traveling a few blocks, the back of the ambulance was plunged into complete darkness.

"We've got a problem," Kerry called back to us. "We've lost our interior and exterior lights and our interior power." That meant no headlights, no lighting for us to work, no suction, no oxygen.

Archie grabbed a flashlight from the wall and shined it on our rear control panel. Using the beam of light as my guide, I switched Henry's oxygen tubing from our onboard oxygen unit back to the small portable tank. "Maybe we can ask the police to give us an escort," I suggested.

"Great idea. We're going to need it," Paula said.

Kerry radioed the patrol cars, and Officer Endicott took the lead in front of us with lights flashing and sirens blaring. Ty, who was driving the medic rig, positioned his vehicle behind us. Hopefully, they'd be able to keep us safely sandwiched between them.

"I need to start an IV, so please shine that light on Henry's arm," Paula said.

Suddenly, the back of the ambulance was flooded with light again. "I was able to get the fifteen-minute fluorescent timer light to work," Jessie said. "It must be on a different circuit."

Now, we had interior lighting but no power. We would be fine without heat or air-conditioning. Since the onboard vacuum no longer worked, I positioned the portable suction unit close to me in case Henry needed it again. What would happen if the ambulance's engine died too?

Henry suddenly coughed out the oral airway. *Another sign that he's waking up more.*

"Go ahead and put a nasal airway in," Paula directed.

A nasopharyngeal (nasal) airway is a tube that is inserted into a person's nasal cavity to help maintain an open airway. It is better tolerated than an oral airway in patients who are semiconscious and need airway protection.

I pulled a container of nasal airways out of an overhead cabinet and chose one that I thought would be the right size. I measured from Henry's ear to the tip of his nose. After coating the airway with a water-based lubricant, I inserted it into his nostril.

After a minute or two, Henry began moving his legs vigorously. Archie tightened the backboard straps so that Henry wouldn't inadvertently harm himself. Jessie continued to provide ventilations with the BVM.

I stroked Henry's head and told him everything was going to be okay. I wasn't sure if he heard me, but I hoped he did and was reassured. A flash of glittering gold around Henry's neck caught my eye. I peered more closely. It was a Miraculous Medal pendant featuring Mary, the mother of Jesus.

At that moment, Henry began breathing on his own. His eyes opened wide. He turned his head and studied my face. After a few seconds, he closed his eyes again.

"Henry, open your eyes," I said. They popped back open. I took his hand in mine. "Squeeze my fingers." Henry gave me a quick, firm squeeze. He understood. He was following simple commands! A sense of awe filled me as I witnessed a miracle unfolding before me.

"How are you feeling?" I asked. Henry looked at me and smiled.

Paula adjusted the flow on the IV line. "I guess you've probably felt better."

Although Henry didn't speak, he chuckled. *A very appropriate response.*

Officer Endicott led us safely to the emergency department parking garage. Kerry backed our rig into one of the parking spots. *We made it.*

As we rolled Henry down the long ED hallway toward room 2, he began speaking. "Where am I? What happened?" With those questions, he showed that his brain was functioning appropriately. Despite the long period of time in which Henry's heart wasn't beating and he couldn't breathe on his own, it appeared that he was going to be cognitively okay.

A swarm of nurses and techs surrounded Henry, and Paula began giving her report to the ER physician.

Life is a precious gift from God. It looked as though Henry was getting a second chance with his. I marveled at how he had collapsed at a wedding—with a skilled physician and automated external defibrillator (AED) only yards away. Judging by the religious medal Henry wore around his neck, I believe that he had placed his faith in the Lord. In turn, God had looked after one of His children.

· · · · · · · · · · · · · ·

The same night we brought Henry into the ED, he underwent an emergency cardiac catheterization and stent placement for a coronary (heart) blockage.

Several weeks later, we learned that Georgette, the pedestrian who had been struck while getting into her car, had suffered a concussion, a tibia (lower leg) fracture, and scapula (wing bone) fracture.

They both made a full recovery.

12

Puddle Jumping

*He jumped to his feet and began to walk. Then
he went with them into the temple courts,
walking and jumping, and praising God.*

ACTS 3:8

We piled into our car after the 8:00 a.m. service at Good Shepherd Church. Almost as soon as we started to drive off, my father said, "I see flashing lights up ahead."

I normally leave my pager in the car during church services. Now, I pressed the replay button to see what I'd missed.

> **DISPATCHER:** "Request for first aid at 218 Hudson Avenue for a 26-year-old female fall victim who fell down a flight of stairs."

I glanced at my watch. The call had been dispatched about 15 minutes ago. I figured the ambulance might be rolling away by the time I got there.

My dad parked behind one of the patrol cars. "We'll wait here until you figure out if they need you."

"Thanks." I headed to the ambulance and peeked through the rear windows. The patient was already inside with Kerry Branson and our new cadet, Scott Jurgenson. Scott, a high school junior, was interested in going into the medical field one day.

I pulled open the rear door. "Need any help?"

Kerry squeezed a bag valve mask, providing rescue breathing to an unconscious female who was strapped onto a backboard. "We sure do. Hop in," Kerry said.

I waved goodbye to my family and stepped into the ambulance. "What can I do?"

"Can you switch over the oxygen from the portable to the onboard unit? The medics should be arriving any minute," Kerry said.

From a glance, our patient appeared to be in critical condition. Bright purple-and-red bruises encircled her right eye.

"Valerie Bloomberg is 26," Kerry said. "She was visiting friends. Last night, she drank a lot of wine and several shots. At one thirty, she fell down an entire flight of stairs. Her friends put her on the sofa so she could sleep it off."

I turned on our suction machine. "That's horrible. Then what happened?"

Kerry paused between ventilations, providing one rescue breath every five seconds. "This morning, her friends tried to wake her up at nine. When they couldn't rouse her, they called 911."

Valerie most likely had suffered a severe traumatic brain injury in the fall. Sadly, lying unconscious on the sofa for eight hours had delayed critical emergency care.

Just then the side door of the ambulance opened, and paramedics Rose Anderson and William Moore entered. While Kerry explained the situation, Rose began intubating Valerie. The process of intubation involves inserting an endotracheal (ET) tube into a person's airway to make it easier to get air into and out of the lungs. Once we got to the hospital, Valerie would be placed on a mechanical ventilator until they could get her medical condition stabilized.

Rose checked Valerie's pupils. One was dilated and the other constricted, pointing to a possible head injury. Valerie's situation was grim. She was clinging to life, but even if she physically recovered, she might have severe brain damage. When we arrived at the emergency department, we rolled Valerie directly into a trauma bay. An experienced team of medical professionals took over her care, and we returned to our ambulance.

Buddy Stone turned up the volume on the ambulance radio. "I think we're about to get another call. I just heard the patrol cars get dispatched for a fall victim." Buddy, a retired pharmaceutical salesman, had been on the rescue squad for about 25 years.

"I was hoping for a chance to eat some breakfast first," Kerry said.

Scott pulled a granola bar out of his pocket. "I can share this with you."

DISPATCHER: "Request for first aid outside the Good Shepherd Church for a 96-year-old fall victim with a head laceration."

"We're going over the Marina Beach Bridge right now. Our ETA is five minutes," Buddy told the dispatcher as he flipped on the emergency lights.

It was a very brisk March morning. I hated the thought of someone that age (or anyone, for that matter) lying on the cold ground. Although the sun was shining after yesterday's mixture of rain and snow, a cold breeze dampened its warming effect.

"I'll grab the trauma kit," I said.

Buddy pulled up alongside a Pine Cove patrol car. Officer Brad Sims was kneeling next to an elderly gentleman, who lay on his left side just where the curb meets the road. Thoughtful bystanders had removed their winter coats and piled them on top of him.

Officer Sims stood up to make room for us to do our assessment. "This is Mr. Golding. He just left church and was walking home."

I was suitably impressed. How many 96-year-olds walk to and from church, especially on a cold winter's morning? I looked at Mr. Golding more closely. He certainly didn't look his age. I'd have guessed him to be closer to 83 or 84.

He had a small laceration above his left eyebrow. There was a hole torn in his trousers near his left knee, revealing an abrasion. His left thumb was also bleeding. He'd probably thrown out his hands to break his fall. I began pulling bandages and dressings out of our trauma kit.

"What happened?" Kerry asked.

Mr. Golding wiggled his feet. "The church service ended, and I was walking home. I tried jumping over this puddle, and my heel must have hit a patch of ice. The next thing I knew, I was tumbling forward." He denied passing out. "Honestly, nothing even hurts. It just stings a bit."

Kerry checked Mr. Golding's pulse, while Buddy and I bandaged his head. We figured we could do the rest of the bandaging in the warm ambulance instead of on the cold pavement. "We're going to take you to the hospital to get checked out," Buddy explained.

Mr. Golding frowned. "I have a family party to go to this evening. How long do you think I'll be at the hospital?"

"You should be home in plenty of time to go to your party," Buddy replied. "We just left the emergency department, and it wasn't busy."

"Very well. Thank you for taking time out of your Sunday to come help me," Mr. Golding said.

I knew Mr. Golding would be fine. The hospital staff would thoroughly clean his wounds and make sure he didn't suffer any fractures or other injuries from the fall. All things considered, he wasn't too much the worse for wear from "puddle jumping."

After we dropped off Mr. Golding at the hospital, I asked veteran triage nurse Maggie Summers if she had any news about Valerie Bloomberg.

"They rushed her into the OR to relieve the pressure on her brain," Maggie said.

It appeared our 96-year-old patient was faring much better from his fall than Valerie, who was 70 years his junior.

. . . .

The next day

I had an open spot at the end of my outpatient physical therapy schedule. I seized the opportunity to run some errands and took an hour of vacation time. I got gas, picked up some wonton soup for dinner, and mailed a package at the post office.

It had drizzled overnight, adding to the slushy mess on the sidewalks. When I got home, I let our dachshund, Schnitzel, run around in the backyard. He charged through the puddles, so I took a few minutes afterward to clean his muddy paws.

．．．．．．．．．．．．．

Terry Guerrero cautiously balanced himself. He glanced down at the mud puddles below. He estimated he was about 35 feet above ground level. That was about 30 feet more than he was comfortable with. He took this job cutting tree limbs because he needed extra cash. He hadn't considered how slippery the branches would be. Or how much he disliked heights.

．．．．．．．．．．．．．

DISPATCHER: "Expedite to 117 Bergen Street for a 46-year-old male fall victim. Man fell 35 feet out of a tree and has a broken arm, broken leg, and other injuries."

Sometimes, we go months without a serious trauma call. Now, it sounded like we were having our second one in two days.

I tossed Schnitzel a tiny dog biscuit and headed to our first aid building. Helen McGuire, Buddy Stone, and Darren Williams arrived at the same time. Darren, retired from a long career with the armed forces, uses much of his free time to volunteer with our squad.

"We're in service to Bergen Street," Helen radioed dispatch.

"Be advised, the paramedics are not available for this call," Dispatcher Jerome Franklin updated us. "As per patrols on the scene, patient is alert and conscious at this time. He's complaining of arm, leg, back, and pelvic pain."

"Thirty-five feet. Yikes. That's over three stories," Buddy noted as he tightened his seat belt.

I donned a pair of purple vinyl medical gloves. "It's amazing he's conscious."

Helen parked in front of a beautiful white Victorian with a wrap-around porch. "It looks like the call is behind the house."

Buddy, Darren, and I lugged our backboard, stabilization equipment, "frac pack" (splinting devices), and first aid bags to the rear of the home. Sergeant Derrick Flint and several workers were squatting around a middle-aged man who lay on his back, squarely in the middle of a large mud puddle.

Sergeant Flint turned toward us. "This is Terry Guerrero. He doesn't know how he fell or what happened. He said one minute he was in the tree, and the next he was on the ground and heard men shouting."

One of the workers had thrown tarps on the ground around Terry. Darren knelt on a tarp close to Terry's head and began holding stabilization to protect his cervical spine. Buddy began performing an assessment, while I checked Terry's vital signs.

"I can't move my left arm," Terry said. "My left foot and back hurt too. I feel the pain all the way into my shoulder blade."

Buddy checked Terry's left arm and shoulder. "We'll need to splint this. His shoulder may be fractured or dislocated. There's tenderness along his left scapula. I can feel a radial pulse on the left."

Terry's arms were large and muscular. I reached into our first aid bag for an extra-large blood pressure cuff and wrapped it around Terry's right upper arm. "His blood pressure is 112 over 72. His pulse is 87, strong and regular, and his pulse ox is 98 percent." It was good his vital signs were normal. Currently, he wasn't showing indications of going into shock.

Buddy slipped a cervical collar around Terry's neck as a precaution, since Terry had fallen such a distance. I tied a knot in the corner of a triangular bandage and placed a sling around Terry's left shoulder. As a team, our crew rolled him onto a backboard to stabilize his spine for the trip to the hospital.

"I sure wish I had passed on this job offer today," Terry told us. "I was trying to make some extra money, but I would have been better off just doing extra hours at my regular job."

"What's that?" Darren asked.

"I design websites. I should probably stick with desk-jockey jobs in the future."

I spread a blanket over Terry to keep him warm. "Well, once they patch you up, you should be able to keep doing your regular job."

Terry shuddered. "My guardian angel must have really had my back today."

We lifted Terry onto our stretcher and rolled him across the grassy yard and into the ambulance. Helen returned to the driver's seat, and Darren slipped into the passenger seat to act as her copilot. Buddy and I climbed into the back to continue caring for Terry. We placed him on oxygen and used shears to cut off his pants and shirt. That way, he was out of his wet, muddy clothing and ready for a full head-to-toe assessment from the trauma surgeon.

When we arrived at Bakersville Hospital, the trauma team met us at the doors. They swept Terry into a trauma bay to begin his care. I reflected on how fortunate Terry was to escape with what appeared to be only orthopedic injuries. His bones would heal with time.

In two days, we'd had just as many first aid calls for men who ended up in mud puddles. Although they required transportation to the hospital, I had no doubt they'd both recover. Valerie's prognosis was more uncertain. I hoped with medical care, therapy, and help from the Lord she would also be well again one day.

13

By the Cross

He is Lord of lords and King of kings—and with him
will be his called, chosen and faithful followers.

REVELATION 17:14

I cranked up my car's heater. A frigid, gale-force wind rocked the sedan. The temperature plunged, with the wind chill making it feel like the single digits. Thick gray clouds blocked any hope of sunshine dispelling the icy chill.

I normally dress in layers but now found myself regretting that I had run out of the house without putting on my thermals. My old snow shovel had broken, and I wanted to pick up a new one at the local variety store. Maybe some more rock salt too.

DISPATCHER: "Request for first aid at the Wesley Avenue Beach for a medical emergency."

I was driving on Wesley Avenue, but in the opposite direction. I did a quick U-turn and flipped on my blue emergency light. The beach was a mere three blocks away.

In my wildest dreams, I couldn't imagine even the most resolute walker venturing out on the boardwalk today. With winds more than

50 miles per hour, coupled with the bitter cold, such a scenario bordered on impossible. So, what kind of emergency could be occurring at the beach? My mind raced with possibilities, but each seemed equally unlikely.

I parked next to a police car and pushed my car door open. The wind caught hold of it, nearly ripping it out of my hand. Officer Jack Endicott was standing near the road. I figured he must be waiting there to direct the ambulance when it arrived on the scene. He pointed to the north. "The call is one block that way. They're about to re-dispatch it with a corrected location."

I rushed along a path that cut through the dunes and led me to the boardwalk. I looked to the left. I didn't see any police officers, but I noticed a hooded figure about a block away, standing on the boardwalk. I jogged toward the person, icy wind blasting my face. I pulled my hood on as I ran, but it blew off again.

I wondered if perhaps someone was having a heart attack or not feeling well. Or perhaps a surfer had been injured in the rough waves. As I rushed along the boardwalk, I looked toward the ocean. There was a large drop-off in the sand just before the shoreline, making it difficult to see far. At first, the beach appeared deserted. I kept searching and finally saw something dark blue past the drop-off. I guessed it must be part of a police officer's uniform.

The person I'd spotted on the boardwalk was a middle-aged man. He was staring out at the ocean, but—perhaps hearing my approaching footsteps—he turned to face me. Hoping he could direct me, I asked, "Is that it?"

He nodded. "I think so." From his answer, I could tell he wasn't sure what was going on either. He had probably seen police officers rush by and had paused to see what was happening.

I sprinted down the flight of stairs and across the sand. As I got closer, I saw that Officer Evan Pearce was in knee-high ocean water, pulling an unconscious man out of the surf and onto the wet sand. Although he was no longer submerged in the frigid ocean, I feared the next wave would strike him. "Get the left arm," Officer Pearce directed.

The next wave hit just as I grabbed the man by the left arm and shoulder. Officer Pearce took hold of his right arm, and Officer Don Woods helped with the legs. We pulled the man far away from the surf to ensure no more waves could wash over him.

I looked more closely at our victim. He was short and slim, small enough that perhaps a blast of wind could have accidentally blown him into the ocean. He was wearing a long, heavy, black winter coat. The weight of that coat must have pulled him down when it became soaked. Wet beige cotton pants clung to his legs. One of his shoes was missing, probably pulled off by the rough surf.

My brain tried to wrap itself around the full horror of the situation I was witnessing. *How is this possible? Why in the world is this elderly man on the beach in frigid temperatures? How could he have made it this far on his own against gale-force winds?*

"He's ice cold," Officer Pearce said.

"And his jaw is stiff," Officer Woods added.

"Do we have any idea how long he's been in the water?" I asked. If we find a person with a stiff jaw under normal conditions, it could be a sign of rigor mortis (rigidity in the muscles due to chemical changes after death). However, this man's stiffness could be due to the bitterly cold water.

"When we got here, we spotted him right away, floating in the water," Officer Woods said. "His downtime couldn't be more than five minutes."

I knelt next to the man's head and slid my index and middle fingers into the groove at the side of his neck to check for a carotid pulse. His face was bluish-purple. "No pulse. Begin CPR."

Officer Pearce unzipped the victim's coat and began performing chest compressions. "One, and two, and three," he counted.

"Don, while I start bagging him, can you set up the defibrillator?" I asked as I unzipped their first aid jump kit and pulled out a bag valve mask. I hooked it up to an oxygen tank and began providing two rescue breaths every time Officer Pearce completed a set of thirty chest compressions.

I used one hand to tilt his head backward to maintain an open airway, and I used the other hand to squeeze the bag against my thigh.

Although I was wearing medical gloves, they were no match for the icy cold. "How did it get called in?" I asked.

"A woman happened to be looking out her window and saw him walking close to the water's edge," Officer Woods replied. "She thought it odd that someone would be walking on the beach in this weather. She got worried and called 911."

"Just as we were arriving, the dispatcher said the caller reported the subject had entered the water," Officer Pearce added. "She said the very first wave knocked him over. He never resurfaced."

Officer Woods quickly prepared the defibrillator. To use one, a person's chest must be dry. We ripped open the victim's shirt and used the sleeves of our coats to dry his chest.

We were racing against the clock, each second precious as we worked to resuscitate him. Although he was clinically dead, we'd keep trying to revive him until his core temperature was brought up to normal. There's an old saying in the realm of first aid: "A person isn't dead until he's warm and dead." As soon as possible, we'd wrap this man in warm blankets and move him into our heated ambulance. Once the paramedics arrived from the hospital, they could administer warm saline via an intravenous drip.

We placed the defibrillator electrodes on the patient's chest, and Officer Woods pressed the analyze button. The machine began whirring. "Shock advised," the automated voice announced.

Officer Woods pressed the shock button. The man's body jerked as joules of potentially life-saving energy entered his body. The defibrillator advised two more shocks, so we gave a stack of three in total.

I rechecked his pulse, hoping I'd now feel a strong one. I didn't. I bit back my disappointment. "Continue CPR."

I glanced over my shoulder and saw the ambulance crew hurrying toward us across the sand. Kerry Branson led the way carrying a first aid bag, while Jessie Barnes and Buddy Stone carried a backboard. Helen McGuire held a pile of blankets, and Darren Williams brought the suction unit and another defibrillator. Jessie and Buddy lined up the backboard next to us and prepared the straps. Darren prepped the suction unit, attaching tubing and running sterile water through it. The officers and I quickly filled them in on what we knew.

"The medics have a five-minute ETA. Let's put him on the backboard and get him into the rig," Jessie said.

The intensely cold wind roared at us. In between giving rescue breaths, I tried twice more to pull my hood back on. Each time, it blew right off. If I was this cold, I shuddered to think how our patient must have felt when his body first contacted the water.

"I need an oral airway," I said. Kerry handed one to me from the first aid kit, and I inserted it into our victim's mouth to help keep his tongue from blocking his airway. Some water bubbled out of the corner of his mouth. Darren suctioned it away using a Yankauer catheter—a hollow, rigid, plastic-tipped device used to aspirate (remove) secretions from the mouth and throat.

Helen piled blankets over the man, leaving just his chest exposed so we could continue to do chest compressions and provide shocks as indicated by the defibrillator. Jessie took over performing chest compressions to give Officer Pearce a break. Although the defibrillator analyzed the patient's heart rhythm several more times, it did not advise giving additional shocks.

Since our patient was small, rather than log-rolling him, we simply lifted him onto the backboard. Helen and Kerry strapped him in while Jessie and I continued to perform CPR. They made sure to strap down the blankets as well.

Then Officers Pearce and Woods, along with Darren and Buddy, performed a four-person lift to carry our patient off the beach. I continued performing rescue breathing as best I could, and Helen followed with the oxygen tank. Somehow, we managed to successfully navigate climbing up the steep, sandy drop-off.

Although the ambulance was a block closer to the scene than where I had parked, there was no easy way to get the backboard from the beach to the road. We'd had a big snowstorm earlier in the week, which had dumped close to a foot of snow. Our town's snowplows had relocated much of the snow to the oceanfront, dumping large amounts along the grassy stretch next to the road. Unfortunately, the snow blocked the sidewalk too. Four men would not be enough to lift our patient up and over the snow mound, so we switched from a four-person to a six-person carry. I lifted one corner of the backboard with my left hand and continued squeezing the BVM with my right.

As soon as we placed the backboard on our stretcher, Kerry began performing a round of chest compressions. We rolled the stretcher into the ambulance.

Helen had had the foresight to make sure the heat was blasting in the back of the ambulance before trekking onto the beach, so it was toasty warm. "We need to cut off these wet clothes as soon as possible," I said. Kerry and Helen worked on cutting off the man's clothing, while Jessie performed chest compressions, and I continued giving ventilations.

Darren went to the driver's seat. He turned his head to speak to us. "The medics are pulling up behind us."

Arthur Williamson and Kennisha Smythe squeezed into the rear of our rig, and I gave them the patient report. "If one of you can drive our ambulance, we can get moving," Kennisha said.

"I will," Helen offered. She slipped out into the cold, and soon we were on our way.

Since water kept spewing from our patient's mouth, Kerry suctioned every minute or two, coordinating with my ventilations. Just when I thought there couldn't possibly be any more water inside him, a little more came out.

Kennisha placed an intraosseous (IO) line into our patient's left tibia bone. An IO line is used to directly infuse medications into bone marrow when an intravenous line is not feasible or possible. Kennisha administered epinephrine through the IO line. Epinephrine, also known as adrenaline, is used to help restart a person's heart.

Arthur put an intravenous line into the man's left arm. He began running warm saline solution through the line in hopes that it would help heat the man's frigid body and improve his hypothermia (low body temperature). Arthur also assessed the patient's heart rhythm. "He's in asystole." Unfortunately, asystole, also referred to as "flatline," is not a shockable rhythm.

Kennisha shifted closer to our patient's head. "I'm going to intubate now. Give him two more good ventilations first."

I squeezed the bag valve mask twice and slid farther back onto the captain's chair to give Kennisha room to work. She deftly inserted an endotracheal tube down the patient's throat. She and Arthur then checked lung sounds, ensuring that the placement of the tube was correct.

As I resumed squeezing the BVM, I noticed our patient wore a striking gold cross around his neck. Numerous small diamonds adorned the top of the filigree pendant. Since my hopes that we'd be able to resuscitate him were dimming, I was comforted by the hint that he was a believer.

Our onboard oxygen alarm began chiming, meaning that our main onboard tank had fallen to less than 500 psi (pounds per square inch). I figured it was because we had two oxygen ports running at 15 liters per minute—one for the BVM, and another providing oxygen via a nasal cannula. I knew we'd still have enough to get us to Bakersville Hospital.

The triage nurse was waiting for us when we arrived. "Take him straight to room 5. Do you have a name?"

Kennisha held the IV line over our patient's head. "Unfortunately, no."

"One of the police officers is following us here. They're working on getting an identification," Helen said.

We moved forward to room 5. As a team, we lifted our patient from our stretcher to the hospital's. I switched the oxygen lines from our portable tanks to the ports on the hospital wall. Within seconds, our patient was surrounded by a physician, respiratory therapist, nurses, and techs.

Someone had placed the man's heavy coat and pants in the basket at the front of our stretcher. I carefully checked each of the pockets in his coat and slacks but didn't find any identification.

As we rolled our empty stretcher out of the hospital, we passed Officer Woods coming in. I hoped he'd discovered the identity of our patient. Outside, we scrubbed down the inside of the ambulance and replaced the equipment we'd used. As we were placing a new sheet on the stretcher, Officer Woods joined us.

"Any luck figuring out who he is?" Darren asked.

"Not exactly. We had a possible lead, since the woman who called 911 said the man's long coat and the way he walked reminded her of a friend. We were able to pull up the driver's license photo of the friend." Officer Woods held up his cell phone. "I showed the picture to the nursing staff, but they couldn't tell if it's the same person. Why don't you take a look?"

Jessie peered at the photo. "I can't tell."

"Maybe, but it's so hard to see," Kerry said.

"It does look like him, but can you scroll the image down?" I asked.

"I sure can." Officer Woods scrolled down.

I felt my heart begin to beat faster. "Now zoom in on the neck area."

Officer Woods zoomed in to the front of the man's neck.

I suddenly felt choked up. "That's him. He's wearing the exact same crucifix." *By the cross. Jesus was with him.*

Darren studied the photo. "What's his name?"

"If this is indeed the person we think it is, his name is Jaxson Milford. He's in his nineties," Officer Woods replied.

Just then, Kennisha stepped outside and joined us. "They're still working on him. They're raising his core temperature right now."

I clung to the hope that Jaxson could still be resuscitated. I turned to Officer Woods. "I just don't understand. Why would such a frail, elderly person venture onto the beach on a day like this?"

"I'm not sure, but it's possible he has dementia," he replied. "He may have gotten lost or confused. The dementia could have impaired his judgment."

My heart went out not only to Jaxson, but also to his friend who had just witnessed such an upsetting tragedy.

"Time to go," Helen said. "We're about to get dispatched for a smell of smoke."

We piled back into the ambulance. During the ride back to Pine Cove, and while we stood by at the fire call scene, my thoughts drifted to Jaxson and how he was doing.

DISPATCHER: "Request for first aid at the Little River Assisted Living Facility for a 92-year-old fall victim with a possible hip injury."

My stomach growled, reminding me I'd never had a chance to get lunch. However, Jaxson's plight dampened my appetite. The fire chief released us from the fire call, so we rolled directly to the assisted living facility.

Darren parked in front of the building. Officer Endicott met us at the front door. "It's going to be an RMA," he informed us. (That means the patient "refused medical attention.") "She said her hip is fine, and she doesn't want to go to the hospital."

Since there were so many of us on the call, Kerry and Jessie went in to assess the patient. The rest of us stayed outside, ready to come in if they needed us.

Kennisha and Arthur pulled up behind us. I walked over to meet them. "We won't need you for this one. It's an RMA," I said.

"Okay. I'm sorry to say I have sad news for you," Kennisha said.

With that, my hopes for Jaxson plummeted. I knew what Kennisha was going to say next.

"They pronounced Mr. Milford right before we left. It was just too much for his heart," Kennisha said.

I reminded myself that Jaxson had had a long life on earth, and the Lord had called him home. His end came quickly, and hopefully he hadn't suffered. He had lived and died wearing Christ's cross, an apparent testimony to his belief in the Lord. I had no doubt he would join Christ in heaven.

14

Going to the Dogs

All the animals and all the creatures that move along
the ground and all the birds—everything that moves on
land—came out of the ark, one kind after another.

GENESIS 8:19

Many years ago, my sister Marie and I walked to the public pool for a beautiful summer's-day dip. When we were still several blocks away, a large German shepherd raced toward us, growling and snarling. I thought we were toast. Just before the dog reached us, he stopped short. With profound relief, I realized he was tethered by a long chain.

After a few hours of fun at the pool, it was time to return home. Marie and I padded along the sidewalk in our flip-flops, wet towels around our necks. All thoughts of our encounter with the ferocious dog earlier that day had long washed away in the swimming pool. Now, they came roaring back.

The German shepherd set upon us from seemingly nowhere: growling, barking, snarling. I reminded myself it was on a lead and wouldn't be able to harm us.

The dog charged us until it was only two feet away, blocking the sidewalk in front of us. *How did it get so close?* With horror, I realized its chain was broken. Only inches separated my sister and me from the dog's vicious fangs. My skinny little body would be no match for the enraged animal.

My heart raced, hammering in my chest. *What can we do?* Running was not an option. There was certainly no sweet-talking this dog. I doubted I'd be able to formulate a coherent word anyway. I imagined we were about to be torn to shreds.

In that moment, God sent us a real-life angel. A small light-blue sedan pulled up next to us, and an older man stepped out. He walked around to the rear of his car, got behind the German shepherd, and picked up the end of its chain.

He looked directly at us, speaking softly and calmly. "Listen closely. I want you to cross around the front of my car. Step into the road to go around the car, and then turn the corner. Once you do that, I want you to run as fast as you can. Don't look back."

We did exactly as he instructed. Once we rounded the corner, I ran as fast as I could. My lungs seared, but I pushed on. As I ran, I could hear ferocious barking. After we ran a block, we turned around to see if the man was okay, but trees and bushes blocked our view. We kept running until we reached home.

Over the years, my sister and I have often thought of our brave rescuer. He fearlessly put his own life at risk to save ours. I shudder to think what would have happened to us had he not intervened. We've always wondered what happened to him after we left. How did he get away? Did he get injured himself? We regretted that we were never able to say a proper thank-you.

Although decades have passed, Marie and I would like to offer a giant, albeit belated, thank-you to our real-life guardian angel for saving our lives.

. . . .

Vincent Packer decided it was time to turn in for the night. He passed through the dining room and headed toward the stairs. He always checked to make sure the gas burners on the stove were turned off before going to bed. Realizing he'd forgotten to do so tonight, he stopped abruptly and turned toward the kitchen. His big toe caught the corner of the rug, causing him to lose his balance. He made a wild grab for the back of one of the dining room chairs, but he missed.

Almost before he realized what was happening, he tumbled toward the floor. His left hip struck first, causing a thunderbolt of pain to shoot across his pelvis.

Vincent broke out in a cold sweat. He knew instantly he wouldn't be able to get up on his own. He needed help. He tried to inch his way to the kitchen, where he had a cordless wall phone.

An hour passed, and he'd only moved six inches. It was no use.

He called for help, hoping a neighbor might hear him. As time passed, his voice grew hoarse. He wished he'd invested in one of those medical alert systems.

. . . .

As I jogged along the boardwalk, a gray haze blocked any hopes of spotting a pristine sunrise. I wouldn't have been able to see it anyway because my pager began beeping.

DISPATCHER: "Request for first aid at 319 Cherry Blossom Lane for a male fall victim with a possible hip injury."

I headed to the first aid building and hopped into the ambulance with Alec Waters and Archie Harris. Our crew parked in front of a small white two-story Colonial with a detached garage. Sergeant Derrick Flint met us at the front door. "Your patient is a 79-year-old male named Vincent Packer. It looks like he's been on the floor since last night because he's incontinent of urine. He's oriented to person and place but not the year. He remembers that his foot caught on the corner of the rug and that he went down hard."

We followed Sergeant Flint through the foyer and kitchen and into a dimly lit living room. "Can we turn some lights on in here?" Alec asked.

Sergeant Flint fiddled with the light switch. "Sorry. This is as bright as it gets."

Although the room was somewhat dark, I could see our patient was an elderly male lying on his back on a black rug such that his legs were partially under the dining room table. Alec interviewed the patient, while Archie began taking vital signs.

Mr. Packer sighed. "I'm so upset with myself. If only I had been more careful."

Alec checked the back of Vincent's head for bumps and lacerations. "Don't beat yourself up. Accidents happen. Who called 911?"

"Vincent's son tried to reach him by phone and was concerned when he didn't pick up. He called us to do a welfare check," Sergeant Flint explained.

I noticed Mr. Packer's left leg was turned outward (externally rotated and shorter as compared to the right leg). This was a sign his left hip could be fractured. "I'll go get the scoop," I said.

While I was outside, I set up our stretcher by the front door. Then I returned to the dining room with the scoop stretcher. Mr. Packer didn't look particularly tall. I guessed the scoop would have to be adjusted to the second notch. I placed it on the floor alongside him to make sure. After I confirmed the necessary length, I knelt near Mr. Packer's right knee to change the length of the scoop.

Suddenly I felt a warm, moist breath on my left cheek. *What in the world?* I quickly scooted backward a few inches, my heart racing.

At that moment, Mr. Packer let out a groan. A few seconds later, I both heard and felt a low rumble coming from underneath the table. I blinked several times, trying to get my eyes to readjust to the dimness after being outside. As I stared at the space under the table, a giant form which had previously blended in with the black rug now became visible.

My voice shook slightly as I asked, "Mr. Packer, do you own a dog?"

"Yes, Maximillian is my Great Dane."

Maximillian, clearly unhappy that we appeared to be inflicting pain on his owner, emitted a long, low growl. The dog easily weighed more than I do. I suppressed a squeal and began slowly easing myself away. I love dogs, but I do not love giant disgruntled dogs that are larger than me. Especially when we are at eye level. "Nice Maximillian. Good doggy."

"I don't think Max would bite you," Mr. Packer said.

His words did not exactly inspire confidence. I mean, sure, Maximillian probably wouldn't devour me if I were merely having a friendly chat with Vincent. But we'd potentially be causing pain as we moved his owner onto our scoop. To make matters worse, we'd then be "stealing him away" to the hospital.

Sergeant Flint found Max's leash on a kitchen hook, as well as dog biscuits in a container on the counter. He tossed him a few biscuits and clipped on the leash while I shined a flashlight on his collar. Using more dog biscuits, Sergeant Flint lured Max out from under the table and into the kitchen.

Without Max breathing down our necks (literally and figuratively), we were able to place Mr. Packer onto our scoop and carry him out to the stretcher. "Don't worry about Max. My son will come get him," he said as we prepared to depart.

I was glad Max had someone to care for him, because Mr. Packer would probably require weeks to recuperate. Now, I make it a habit to glance under tables before diving into first aid calls!

. . . .

It was just past eleven o'clock at night. I returned from a late-night first aid call to find our Belgian shepherd, Montana, waiting for me at the front door.

I figured Montana's bladder was brimming. I flipped on the backyard light switch and slid open the patio door. The floodlights illuminated the right side of the deck and yard, but the left bulb had burned out the previous week. We hadn't had a chance to change it yet, so the left section of the deck was dark.

Montana rushed out the door. Normally, she zips off to the right and down the stairs into the grassy yard. This time, she turned to the left and disappeared into the darkness.

Puzzled, I called out her name. She returned, pushed her nose into my thigh, and rushed away. I followed and found her standing at the far corner of the deck. She whined as I got closer and sniffed something on the deck.

I pulled her back by the collar so I could see what held her interest.

It was a small brown sparrow struggling to free itself. The toes of its right foot were caught between the boards of our deck. I love birds, and my heart filled with compassion. I wondered how long the little guy had been trapped.

DISPATCHER: "Request for first aid for a young sparrow with a possible leg injury; expedite due to entrapment."

The call wasn't really dispatched on my pager. But if it had been, that's what I imagined the dispatcher would say. I brought Montana inside so she wouldn't inadvertently give the bird a heart attack. Then I grabbed a flashlight and headed back outside.

I knelt next to the sparrow. Speaking softly, I slipped my fingers into the crack between the boards. I hoped I could free the bird quickly. But what if I couldn't? What if he was truly stuck? What if he had a broken leg?

Anxiously, the sparrow began fluttering his wings, which made it more difficult to see his leg. Several long moments passed as I struggled to free the bird. It seemed so tiny, so defenseless. I continued to wiggle and jiggle his leg as best I could. After several more minutes, the leg popped loose. I sheltered the sparrow in my hands, trying to give him a chance to recover.

As I held him, I hoped he would both warm up and calm down. Having a large dog snuffle him and human hands manipulate him after being trapped for possibly hours must have been nothing short of terrifying. After a short while, I placed him on our deck railing and held my breath.

The sparrow stood for several seconds, seemingly able to bear weight through his legs without a problem. Then he flew up and away, landing on the branch of one of our holly trees.

If it hadn't been for the late-night first aid call, I would have been asleep. If Montana hadn't met me at the door, I wouldn't have let her out. If she hadn't gone out, she wouldn't have led me to the sparrow. I honestly don't think the bird would have survived the cold night on our deck. Even if he had, I wouldn't have ever found him there without Montana leading me to him.

On that night, many pieces had to fall together for us to help rescue one of God's tiniest creatures.

PS: Montana got extra dog biscuits that night for her excellent search and rescue work.

15

The Unexpected

*They also will answer, "Lord, when did we see you
hungry or thirsty or a stranger or needing clothes
or sick or in prison, and did not help you?"*

MATTHEW 25:44

y father adjusted his rearview mirror. "We'll stop at the next exit
for dinner. If I recall correctly, there's a little Italian restaurant
there."

"Let's try to make it quick," my mom said. The forecast called for
light rain, and she was concerned about the possibility of black ice.

"Sounds good," I said, pausing the DVD player. We were on our
way home from visiting relatives. After a long and busy day, I was looking forward to going to bed.

Within a half hour, the three of us were seated in a cozy restaurant near a crackling fireplace. The smells of oregano and garlic wafted
through the air. After we ordered, I gazed at my surroundings. About
half of the tables were occupied. I surmised that some of the custom-
ers were locals, and the rest were probably travelers like us.

Our waitress started us out with a warm loaf of Italian bread and
side salads. I savored the taste of a thick slice of bread dipped in olive
oil. My parents and I chatted about what we still needed to do before
Christmas, like shopping, baking cookies, and picking a tag from the
giving tree at church.

The waitress served our main course, and I took a few bites of lasagna. Suddenly, I heard a commotion at the table next to us. I turned to my left just as an elderly woman screamed, "My husband needs help!"

I sprang to my feet and rushed to them. "What's wrong?"

The woman grabbed my forearm. "I think he's having a heart attack."

I squatted next to a man who looked to be in his eighties. He was hunched forward in his chair. His face was turning blue, indicating he wasn't getting enough oxygen. His eyes were wide with fear. Was he indeed having a heart attack? Or could he be choking?

"Sir, can you speak? Are you choking?" I asked. He didn't reply.

It was clear he couldn't get any air into his lungs. I squatted behind his chair and wrapped my arms around his midsection. I began performing abdominal thrusts, fervently praying that the Heimlich maneuver would dislodge whatever was stuck in his throat.

Approximately 4,000 people die from choking in the United States each year. In fact, it's the fourth leading cause of unintentional death in our country. Only about 25 percent of choking victims who fall unconscious or become unresponsive receive chest compressions from a bystander. Why such a low number? Perhaps people don't know how to help. Maybe they don't recognize that the person is choking. If someone at the scene doesn't know the Heimlich maneuver, victims must wait until EMS arrives. Unfortunately, this means survival rates go down.

I heard a waitress say she was calling 911. The couple seated across the table from the choking victim began praying. At that point, I blocked out everything else. Time seemed to stand still. All that existed in my world was my mission to dislodge the foreign object from the man's airway.

He began slouching farther forward, and I feared he was going unconscious from lack of oxygen. As I gave the gentleman more abdominal thrusts, a chunk of steak shot out of his mouth and onto the table in front of him.

He immediately began breathing, sucking life-saving air into his oxygen-starved lungs. I felt his radial pulse at the thumb-side of his wrist. It was strong and regular. The bluish hue of his face morphed into a healthy pink.

The waitress rushed over to the table. "EMS is on the way."

The gentleman nodded. "I don't think I've ever been more scared in my life, but I feel much better now. Thank you so much. The steak went down the wrong way and got stuck."

I continued to kneel next to him. "I'm glad you're feeling better now. Your pulse and breathing rate are normal. When the paramedics get here, they'll examine you, and they can take you to the hospital to get checked out."

As the medics arrived, I stood up to get out of the way. The man's wife hugged me tightly. "Thank God you were here."

I returned her hug. "I'm glad I could help."

I slipped back into my seat next to my parents. Knowing how to assist choking victims is a topic that's near and dear to my heart. The first time I ever performed the Heimlich maneuver on someone, it wasn't during a first aid call. It was on my own father.

I reflected that choking or witnessing someone else being unable to breathe is a wake-up call for all of us. It reminds us of the fragility of life. If you have relationships to mend with God or family, don't push it off until tomorrow. Vow to start repairing them today.

A short time later, we settled into our car to finish the last leg of our journey.

"On our way out of the restaurant, I overheard a woman tell the person she was sitting with that you just saved a man's life," my mom said. (She's my mother, so of course she was feeling super proud of me at that moment.)

I knew who deserved the credit, and it wasn't me. It belonged to a higher power. God had placed us in that restaurant at precisely the right time for me to be able to assist. We could have saved time by going to a fast-food restaurant, but my father chose that little Italian restaurant instead. I marveled at how once again the Lord had set the pieces in motion to orchestrate a rescue. He so often intervenes in quiet ways to help us. I felt truly blessed to have had the opportunity to assist someone in need.

· · · · · · · · · · · · ·

We finally got to bed in the wee hours of the morning. When my pager woke me up before six o'clock, I felt groggy. Our dog had woken me up several times during the night because he urgently needed to go out due to bouts of diarrhea. I sneezed several times, and my nose started running. I hoped my seasonal allergies weren't acting up.

> **DISPATCHER:** "Request for first aid for an 85-year-old female who is not feeling well. Exact location of the call is being determined."

I slipped on my shoes and donned a heavy coat. My father had parked our car in the garage to keep it out of the rain. I pulled the driver's seat forward, started the engine, and threw the gear into reverse. As I began backing up, I heard what sounded like running water. Could the car be leaking fluids? To sound like that, it would have to be a *lot* of fluids.

Next, I heard a rattling noise followed by a banging noise. It sounded like I was dragging something underneath the car. Could we have accidentally picked up a branch on the drive home last night? Was it stuck under the car and now grinding along the driveway pavement? If so, I knew I needed to pull it out. I recalled a friend once telling me that he accidentally got a plastic bag stuck under his car, and it caught on fire. I knew I should probably put the car in park and check underneath, but I didn't want to be late for the first aid call. The sound subsided. Maybe I could see what was wrong after the call.

I backed up several more feet to see if the odd noises returned. Suddenly, I heard a male voice coming from the rear of the car. My heart pounding, I slammed on the brakes. I whipped my head around to see who was in our car.

No one. There's no one there. What in the world is going on?

Had I somehow accidentally dialed my parents on my cell phone? It was a male voice, but it sure didn't sound like my dad.

Now, I heard a second male voice. It almost seemed as though I was listening in on someone else's conversation. But how was that possible? Were there men standing outside my car? But why would they be on our driveway? And they sounded threatening.

Suddenly, I recognized the voices. Apparently, when I had started the car, our *Home Alone* DVD had automatically begun playing from where it had left off the previous evening. My moments of fear melted away into sheepishness. Now, it was truly time to answer the first aid call.

16

The Journey

Show me, LORD, my life's end
and the number of my days;
let me know how fleeting my life is.

PSALM 39:4

*I*t won't be long now. I'm getting weaker and weaker. Dawn Rivers's doctor had told her and her husband, Dante, that she only had a few weeks left to live. The news hadn't surprised her. Deep down, she'd already suspected as much. She had advanced stage IV breast cancer. She'd been battling the disease for eight years and had exhausted all treatment options. Last week, her doctor had suggested she consider hospice.

Dawn and Dante had been married for 42 years. They met just after college when they both joined the church choir. Dante asked Dawn out for coffee after choir practice one evening. Within six months, they were engaged. Five months later, they walked down the aisle together. The entire choir sang at their wedding, rejoicing in their love for each other and Christ.

Dawn had come to terms with the finality of her disease months ago, carried by her strong faith in the afterlife. Now, she was only hanging on for Dante's sake. He told her almost every day that he couldn't bear the thought of living without her.

She had tried her best to console him. "You'll be okay. You have our kids." Their children were grown, but they lived in the area.

Now, Dawn used the remote control to elevate the head of her hospital bed a little more. Every bit of exertion seemed to fatigue her lately. Her arms and legs were swelling, too, which made it even harder to move them. Licking her lips, Dawn eyed the glass of water on the small table next to her bed.

Just then, Dante came in. "Oh, let me get that for you," he said, knowing what she wanted without her having to say a word. They had always been like that.

She smiled to ease some of his anxiety. "Thanks."

With each day that passed, it was obvious that Dante grew more worried. He lovingly brushed a strand of hair from Dawn's forehead. "Your skin feels warm. Do you have a fever?" Before she could answer, he rushed out of the room, likely to get a thermometer from the bathroom vanity.

Dawn watched his retreating figure, and a rush of love for him swept over her. *I've been so incredibly blessed. Lord, please look after Dante when I'm gone.*

Dante reappeared with a thermometer and gently placed it under Dawn's tongue. "It's 102.5. I'm calling the doc right away." He strode into the kitchen to use the phone.

Dawn closed her eyes, only half listening to Dante's side of the conversation with her oncologist. She preferred to stay home, but if it made her husband feel better, she was willing to go to the hospital. The sound of his voice comforted her, and she drifted off into a restless sleep.

· · · · · · · · · · · · ·

DISPATCHER: "Request for first aid at 622 Jefferson Avenue for an oncology patient with a fever."

I recognized the address and sighed, trying to brush away the glumness that crept into my heart. I'd taken Dawn Rivers to the hospital about a month ago, a few weeks before Thanksgiving.

Alec Waters, Colleen Harper, and I arrived with the ambulance at the Jefferson Avenue home a few minutes later. Dante, a sprightly man with warm brown eyes, met us at the front door.

I readjusted the position of the first aid bag's strap on my shoulder. "Hi, Mr. Rivers. I'm sorry to hear that your wife isn't feeling well today."

Dante patted me on the shoulder. "Thanks for coming out for us. It seems like we've been seeing a lot of you lately."

We found Dawn sleeping in her hospital bed, toward the back corner of the living room. She had told me once that she liked having the bed there because she could see the bird feeder in their backyard. Hearing our voices, she roused from her nap. "Oh, hi everyone. Sorry to bring you out again. You probably have better things to do."

"Don't be silly. That's what we're here for," Colleen said. She began checking Dawn's vital signs, while I filled out the call sheet. I recalled most of the information from the last first aid call, but I had to ask her husband to remind me of her date of birth. Next, we positioned her onto our Reeves (collapsible stretcher) and then shifted her onto our cot. Soon, we were loaded in the ambulance and ready to take off for the emergency room.

"I have to find my glasses. I'll pack a few things and meet you there," Dante said. He blew a kiss through the back door of the ambulance. My heart clenched as Dawn smiled and blew one back to him.

"I'm so worried about Dante," Dawn confided. "He's terrified of letting go. But look at me, girls. We all know that it's almost my time. My doctor said that I probably only have a few weeks left to live."

I couldn't formulate any words. Instead, I squeezed her hand, wishing I could take away some of the pain and worry.

Dawn caught sight of my stricken face. "It's okay. I feel at peace. I'm ready to go."

"We just wish there were something more we could do," Colleen said.

"Oh, you girls have helped enough. Maybe it's just as well I'm going to the hospital today. Tomorrow, Dante is taking the train into the city.

He must take care of a little business there. One of my children was going to come and sit with me for the day, but if I get admitted, they won't have to. You know, I hate to be a burden."

I smoothed the blanket around Dawn's shoulders. "Judging from the way your husband looks at you, I don't think he'd ever consider you a burden. And I'm sure your kids feel the same."

Dawn smiled and closed her eyes, and we lapsed into silence. She stirred as we lifted her out of the ambulance. "My goodness, are we here already? That was fast."

We rolled Dawn through the doors to the emergency room, and I found myself wondering if she would ever return home. I knew that she and her husband had enjoyed 42 magical years together, but with the end now in sight, it probably didn't seem nearly long enough to them.

. . . .

The next day

Dante reread the newspaper headline for the third time, without knowing what he had just read. He felt distracted and jittery, eager to get home and hurry to the hospital to visit Dawn. His business in the city had taken a little longer than expected, and he was anxious for the train to arrive in Pine Cove. He glanced at his wristwatch. *Three more stops. I'm almost home.*

His mind wandered back to his wife, and the perpetual heaviness that he always felt in his heart nowadays seemed magnified somehow. *How will I go on, Lord? How can I live without her?* Caught in a web of frustration and despair, he'd struggled with these questions for the past several months. He knew Dawn seemed at peace with her destiny, and he wished he could have even a fraction of her acceptance.

"Next stop, Pine Cove," the conductor said, interrupting Dante's reflections. Wearily, he grabbed his briefcase and moved toward the back of the train car.

. . . .

DISPATCHER: "Request for first aid at the train station for a fall victim."

Darren Williams took the wheel, and Mason Chapman, Buddy Stone, and I climbed into the back of the ambulance. Just then, our pagers went off again.

DISPATCHER: "Expedite. CPR in progress."

The ambulance surged forward, and I grasped the overhead bar to steady myself. Reaching into the cabinet with my other hand, I grabbed the suction unit and airway kit. Mason grasped the defibrillator. It crossed my mind that Dante Rivers had taken the train into the city today, but I brushed the thought aside.

Darren parked by the curb close to the station. A crowd had formed on the platform, and we figured that's where we would most likely find our patient. We caught sight of police uniforms and rushed through the crowd toward them.

On the way there, I overheard a bystander say, "That poor man's wife is dying of cancer."

I suppressed a shiver. *No way. Please don't let it be Dante Rivers.*

Officer Brad Sims was performing chest compressions, while Officer Jack Endicott was providing rescue breathing with a bag valve mask to an older gentleman, who lay on his back on the brick pavement. I was almost afraid to look at the victim's face.

Officer Sims glanced up at us. "It's a witnessed arrest. He collapsed getting off the train, and a bystander started CPR immediately. We tried to defibrillate, but no shock was advised." The fact that it was a witnessed arrest meant that someone saw the man collapse. That increased his chance of survival.

I knelt by the man's head to insert an oral airway. With tangible relief, I noted he wasn't Dante Rivers. I held the oral airway up to the man's face, measuring from the tip of his ear to the corner of his mouth.

After I inserted it, I held the bag valve mask steady on his face while Officer Endicott continued squeezing the bag.

Buddy fished around in our patient's pocket and pulled out his wallet. He glanced at the contents. "His name is Richard Randolph. He's a local."

We interrupted chest compressions just long enough to roll the man onto a backboard. The crowd parted as we rolled the stretcher to our ambulance.

Paramedics Rose Anderson and William Moore climbed into the rig with us. They attached their heart monitor and defibrillation pads to Richard's chest.

Rose studied the heart monitor. "It's a non-shockable rhythm. He's in asystole. Continue CPR."

My hopes for resuscitation began fizzling like a leaky hot-air balloon sinking quickly from the sky and heading for rocky ground. William positioned himself at Richard's head. "I'll intubate."

Rose nodded in agreement and began establishing an intravenous line so she could administer potentially life-saving medications. When she was done, she looked at the ECG again. "I've got V-fib on the monitor. I'm going to shock him. Everybody clear." She waved her arm over Richard's body to make sure no one was touching him when she pressed the shock button. His body shuddered in response to the shock, and I found myself holding my breath as William checked for a carotid pulse.

"No pulse. Continue chest compressions," William said.

Once again, my hopes plummeted. Mason resumed chest compressions. I resumed squeezing the BVM, praying for a miracle.

When we arrived at the emergency room, a physician and team of nurses ushered us into the code room (a special room where we take patients who are in cardiac arrest). As I switched the oxygen from our portable unit to the hospital's supply, a sadness settled across my chest. I knew Richard wasn't going to make it. Too much time had already passed. If he were somehow resuscitated now, he'd have severe brain damage. In my heart, I knew that the ER staff would probably pronounce him before we even left the hospital.

• • • • • • • • • • • • •

Over the next several days, my mind drifted at times to thoughts of Dawn Rivers. About two weeks after we took her to the hospital, I saw her name in the obituaries. I recalled Dawn's words in the back of the ambulance: *"I feel at peace. I'm ready to go."* I hoped Dante would eventually come to terms with his loss. I took comfort in knowing that Dawn had had a happy life with Dante and her family. Now, it was time for the next leg of her journey—eternal life with Christ.

17

Preserving Memories

*Timothy has just now come to us from you and has brought
good news about your faith and love. He has told us
that you always have pleasant memories of us and that
you long to see us, just as we also long to see you.*

1 THESSALONIANS 3:6

One chilly autumn evening, Colin Branigan—a member of the
Pine Cove First Aid Squad—and his wife, Lauren, were clean-
ing dinner dishes in their kitchen. Lauren paused while drying a plate.
"Do you smell gas?"

Colin didn't get a chance to respond because someone began banging loudly on their front door. When he pulled the door open, he saw
three children running away. Puzzled, he stepped outside to see what
they were doing. He heard a crackling noise coming from the area of
his neighbor's house. To his horror, he discovered their front porch was
engulfed in flames. He pulled his cell phone from his back pocket and
dialed 911. "I need the fire department at 304 Daisy Drive..."

. . . .

My family and I were visiting my sister Marie for dinner. "Does
anyone want seconds?" she asked. We were enjoying a tasty meal of
chicken drumsticks, stuffing, and corn.

Before I could reply, my pager went off.

DISPATCHER: "Request for the fire department and first aid squad at 304 Daisy Drive for a working structure fire."

It had been a busy day for our first aid squad. In the morning, we had taken an elderly woman who felt dizzy to the hospital. A little while later, we'd had a call for a middle-aged man with chest pains. After that, we had stood by for a fire alarm at a local hotel. Now, it seemed like our night would be just as busy as our day had been.

"Sorry, we have to go. How about dessert for the road?" I asked, never one to pass up a sweet treat.

Marie passed me a cookie, and I tucked it carefully into my pocket. As soon as the sun had set a few hours ago, an autumn chill had caused the thermometer to dip into the forties. A cool breeze would make it feel even colder. I wished I'd brought a warmer coat with me.

Marie, reading my mind, tossed me one of her fleece hoodies. "Maybe you can put that on underneath your jacket."

"Thanks so much." I knew I'd be glad to have the extra layer. Fire calls normally last for hours. It would only grow colder as the night wore on.

We said a quick goodbye, and my family drove me to the scene. The entrance to Daisy Drive was completely blocked, so they dropped me off at the nearest intersection. Flashing red lights from numerous fire trucks lit up the street.

As I jogged toward the fire, the acrid stench of smoke filled the air. Big clouds of black smoke billowed into the evening sky. When I drew closer, I could see that the front of the house was fully engulfed in flames.

Skilled firefighters trained their hoses on the raging inferno. Pine Cove boasts some of the bravest and most highly trained firefighters I know. They were doing everything in their power to beat back the flames.

Two of our ambulances were parked far enough away from the fire to leave room for the fire trucks. I passed by the house and joined Colin Branigan, Jessie Barnes, Buddy Stone, Kerry Branson, and Darren Williams.

"I can't believe it. My wife smelled gas, and then there was banging on our front door." Colin related seeing children running away, discovering the blaze, and alerting 911. "I told the police about the kids. It turns out they were going door to door selling magazines. They saw the blaze and were banging on doors to get help."

"Thank goodness you came out when they knocked and noticed the fire. Are the owners okay?" I asked.

Colin zipped up his coat. "They aren't home, but I heard that the police located them, and they're on their way here."

I couldn't imagine their devastation when they realized everything they owned was destroyed. "Do they have any pets?"

"A cat," Colin replied.

I know cats are resourceful, but I wasn't sure any living creature could survive that kind of fire. My heart clenched with sympathy for the family.

A large crowd of neighbors gathered in the surrounding yards to watch. The firefighters worked diligently, risking their own lives. Within a half hour, they knocked down the fire. One firefighter, Steve, scalded his neck, so he came to us for first aid treatment. We brought him into the ambulance. "The fire was so intense that it burned the service wire off the house," he said.

"Well, at least you don't have to worry about electric wires on the ground," Jessie replied.

Darren applied a cold pack to soothe Steve's neck. "It looks like it's a minor burn."

"Any idea what caused the fire?" Buddy asked.

"It looks like it's probably electrical, but the fire marshals will conduct an investigation to make sure."

"If you need us to take another look at your burn, or if you need another ice pack, you know where to find us," Darren said.

Steve stood up. "Thanks, everyone. I'm sure I'll be fine. I want to go back over there and start working again."

Part of me didn't want to know the answer, but I asked anyway. "Do you know if the cat is okay?"

Steve shook his head. "I'm sorry to say the poor little guy didn't make it."

I wasn't surprised by the news, but I was saddened by it.

From where we stood across the street from the fire, we watched the family arrive. A short while later, the homeowner approached us. "Hi, I'm Anita. I just want to thank you for all you've done."

Surrounded by so much devastation, I was amazed that Anita even thought of us. And anyway, I felt like I hadn't really done anything to deserve thanks. I would have loved to have been able to help in a more meaningful way.

Anita stared across the street at the remains of her house. "Now that the fire's out, I wonder if they would let me go inside to look around. Maybe there's something left that hasn't been ruined."

I hoped so for her sake, but the situation looked grim. The porch and front part of the house had been destroyed. Even if some of their belongings had survived the fire, they could have easily been damaged by smoke and water.

Jessie pointed to Fire Chief Ray Watson. "He might be able to answer your question."

Although the breeze quieted, the temperature continued to drop as time slipped by. My teeth chattered. I wrapped a thin white first aid blanket around my legs to warm up.

"I just heard that Chief Watson sent in a few of the firefighters to see if anything is salvageable," Colin said.

"It sure would be nice if they could save something," I replied.

Jessie crossed his fingers. "Let's hope so."

A short while later, Anita approached us again. "I just wanted to let you know, those firefighters are amazing. They were able to pull out two of our family photo albums."

"That's terrific," Buddy said.

"The only problem is the albums are soaking wet. I'm afraid the photos may have been destroyed. Or if they aren't yet, they will be. They're the old-fashioned kind of albums, you know, with the peel-back plastic sheets. The photos are incredibly old, so I'm not sure they'll survive," Anita said.

"Are those the albums in your arms?" Darren asked.

Anita held them up for us to see. "Yes, I'm carrying them around with me to make sure nothing happens to them."

"I have an idea," Kerry said. "We're just waiting for the fire department to finish. Why don't you give them to us? We can dry them off."

"Oh, I couldn't possibly impose on you like that," Anita protested.

"We insist," Buddy said.

"We'd love to help," I added.

Chief Watson called Anita's name. She handed Kerry the albums. "I can't thank you enough," she said before walking toward the chief.

I pulled off the white blanket from around my waist and laid it down on the grass. Jessie got the flashlights out of the rig, and Buddy got several more blankets and a pile of towels. As a team, we painstakingly removed each photo from the albums. Although a few were dry, many were damp or soaked. We took great care not to accidentally tear any as we placed each one on a blanket. There were childhood portraits, holiday and vacation photographs, and tickets to special events. I noticed some paper currency from foreign countries and figured the bills were probably mementos from family vacations. We pressed each with a first aid towel to remove the moisture.

Soon, we had two large blankets full of old photographs. I realized Anita and her family had lost many possessions that night. I was glad we could help save some priceless photos. I hoped they would provide Anita and her family a small measure of comfort. Even in the darkest times, Jesus shines a light.

Our rescue squad served a unique function that night. Instead of providing first aid to living people, we preserved memories.

18

Keeping the Faith

*This calls for patient endurance on the part of the people of
God who keep his commands and remain faithful to Jesus.*

REVELATION 14:12

bicycled around Pine Cove Lake and throughout town, enjoying the
fall foliage and mild temperature. When my pager went off, I ped-
aled as fast as I could to our first aid building.

> **DISPATCHER:** "Request for first aid at 2019 Kingston Avenue for a
> 66-year-old female with a possible broken hip."

When I arrived at the squad building, Colleen Harper was already
pulling the ambulance out onto the front apron. Ted O'Malley sat
next to her. I stashed my bike behind the building and hopped into
the back of the rig.

Colleen picked up the mic. "We're in service. Any additional
responding members can meet us at the scene."

"Received," Dispatcher Jerome Franklin replied. "Patrols on the
scene report that the patient is alert and conscious at this time, complaining of left hip pain."

Colleen pulled up in front of a white Cape Cod–style home. A beautiful Japanese maple tree with luscious red leaves adorned the front lawn. We swept past it on our way into the house.

Officer Vinnie McGovern met us in the foyer. "The call is for Julia Christensen. She slipped on the hardwood floor in the living room. She said she went down hard but never lost consciousness."

When I rounded the corner into the living room, I spotted Julia. She was crumpled on her left side with her back to us. A man with short gray hair, whom I assumed to be her husband, hovered close by. I noticed Julia's left leg was significantly shorter than the right and turned outward (externally rotated), which indicated a possible hip fracture.

"If you want to start getting a set of vital signs, I'll get the scoop," Ted suggested to Colleen and me, referring to our scoop stretcher.

"Thanks," Colleen replied. Then she knelt next to Julia and introduced us. I passed Colleen a blood pressure cuff, stethoscope, and pulse oximeter.

As Colleen assessed Julia, I began to write up the patient call sheet. I turned to the gentleman. "May I ask you some questions?"

"Yes, I'm Julia's husband, Nicholas. She's the healthy one. She really doesn't have any medical problems except osteoporosis. In fact, she's the one who takes care of me. You can check with her yourself to make sure I'm not forgetting something."

As Colleen called out Julia's vital signs, I recorded them on the run sheet. They were all normal. Fortunately, nothing appeared injured except her hip.

When Ted returned with the scoop, we carefully placed Julia on it. Throughout the ordeal, she appeared more concerned about Nicholas than herself. "Don't come with me to the hospital, honey. You should stay home. I'm sure I'll be fine."

Nicholas's anxiety showed clearly on his face. "Okay, if you think that's best, but please keep me posted."

As soon as we loaded Julia into the ambulance, her cell phone rang. "It's my daughter Sue. I don't feel like talking right now. Could you please explain to her what's going on?"

I reached for the phone. "Of course." I explained to Sue that her mother had fallen and possibly broken her hip. "They'll give her pain medication and take X-rays."

Sue lived locally. "Please tell my mother I'll meet her at the hospital in fifteen minutes. And tell her not to worry about Dad."

When I relayed the message to Julia, she smiled. "I'm the one who cares for everyone else. And prays for everyone else. Now, I need someone to pray for me."

Colleen clasped her hand. "You have two people right here who are praying for you. And it sounds like your family is too."

Given Julia's level of pain and the way her leg was unnaturally turned out, she most likely had a fracture and would need surgery. We transferred her care to the staff of the Bakersville ED. I hoped for a rapid recovery.

. . . .

Six days later

My evening work meeting was canceled. I decided to use the found time to vacuum. I switched my pager to the vibrate mode in case we received a call. Before I could finish cleaning the kitchen, my pager began buzzing.

DISPATCHER: "Request for first aid at 2019 Kingston Avenue for a 68-year-old male, unresponsive but breathing. Possible stroke."

After hurrying over to the squad building, I climbed into the ambulance next to our driver, Archie Harris, and strapped on my seat belt. "We had a call at this residence about a week ago. A woman fell and hurt her hip. This sounds like the call might be for her husband," I said.

Mason Chapman climbed into the rear of the ambulance. "Archie, I'm all set back here. You can go."

DISPATCHER: "Update: Expedite as per patrols on scene."

Archie flipped on the lights and sirens, and we were on our way. Cars pulled to the side of the road to get out of the way, and Archie deftly maneuvered around them.

I pulled on a pair of medical gloves. "It's the white Cape Cod on the right."

Mason and I grabbed our essential rescue equipment and hustled into the house. Nicholas Christensen lay on his back on the kitchen floor, close to the breakfast table. His eyes were closed, his face ghostly pale. At a glance, I could see he was critically ill. A woman in her thirties stood close by. I assumed it was his daughter Sue, whom I had spoken to on the phone last week regarding her mother, Julia.

Officer Kyle Jamieson was setting up a bag valve mask (BVM). Intelligent and trustworthy, Officer Jamieson was moving up the ranks toward sergeant. "His respiratory rate is only 6." A normal breathing rate is 12 to 20 breaths per minute. A rate of 6 is dangerously low, requiring supplemental help with a BVM.

"I couldn't get a radial pulse," Sergeant Derrick Flint said. If he couldn't feel a pulse, that meant Nicholas's systolic blood pressure was critically low.

I knelt by Nicholas and palpated along the side of his neck for a carotid pulse. I could feel it, but it was weak. While Officer Jamieson performed rescue breathing, giving one breath every five seconds, I took a quick blood pressure reading. "It's only 70 over 50." I turned to Sue. "I need you to tell me exactly what happened."

"My mother broke her hip and is in a rehab center. I stopped by to check on Dad. When I came in, I found him just like this. I called 911 right away," she said.

"Please tell me about your dad's medical history. Is he a diabetic? Has he ever had a heart attack or stroke?" I asked.

"He had a ministroke last year. He hasn't felt great for the past three days. I thought it was because he was missing Mom. But when I found him on the floor, I thought he might be having a stroke," Sue explained.

"How about medications?" I grabbed several pill bottles off the kitchen table and read one of the labels. "Is this his oxycodone?"

"Yes, he takes that for back pain. He hurt his back a few weeks ago," Sue replied.

I gently pulled open Nicholas's eyelids and peered at his pupils. *Constricted, bordering on pinpoint.* "The oxycodone bottle is empty. Could your father have intentionally overdosed?"

Sue nervously ran a hand through her long blond hair. "No, he would never do that. But…"

I paused from measuring an oral airway to look at her. "But what?"

"He could have done it accidentally. My mom takes care of his medications. With her in the rehab center, it's possible he could have gotten confused."

Mason set up the portable suction unit in case we needed it. The defibrillator stood next to it, ready to be used in case Nicholas's heart stopped beating.

I tried to insert the oral airway, but Nicholas gagged, so I inserted a nasal airway instead. The opioid overdose triad includes slowed breathing or respiratory arrest, pinpoint pupils, and unconsciousness or unresponsiveness. Nicholas's pupils weren't pinpoint, but they were constricted. His breathing effort was decreased, and he was both unconscious and unresponsive. My gut told me that he'd overdosed.

At the time, police departments and EMS squads didn't carry naloxone (Narcan), the antidote to an opioid overdose. We'd need the paramedics for that. I turned to Sergeant Flint. "What's the ETA on the medics?"

He radioed headquarters. "They're five minutes out."

"We have time to get him in the rig before they get here. Let's put him on the backboard," Mason said.

We rolled Nicholas onto a backboard and buckled the straps. Mason and Sergeant Flint carried him outside and placed the backboard on the stretcher, while I walked alongside them and squeezed the BVM. As we wheeled Nicholas to the ambulance, a soft rain began falling.

Sue squeezed my shoulder. "I'm going to leave now to drive to the hospital. I'll meet you there."

"Okay, we'll see you in a bit." I knew that Nicholas's life was in the balance, and he needed advanced life support right away. The medics could administer life-saving naloxone. Would they get here in time?

I switched the portable oxygen to the onboard tank while Mason squeezed the BVM. Soon, two paramedics with whom I was not familiar entered the rig. I read their name tags: *Brenda Nielsen* and *Frederick Dixon*. Right away, I said, "This is very important. I think he needs Narcan. He may have overdosed on his oxycodone by accident."

Frederick pulled a penlight out of his breast pocket and shined it into Nicholas's eyes. "No, this is not a Narcan case."

Just like that, Frederick dismissed me. For a second, I doubted myself. Could it be something else other than an overdose? A stroke, perhaps? A force deep within told me to have faith in myself and push harder for Narcan. "No, really. His wife oversees his medications, and she's in the hospital right now. His daughter said it's possible he could have gotten confused and taken the wrong dose."

"He doesn't have pinpoint pupils," Frederick pointed out.

"But they are constricted," I persisted. "I really think he needs Narcan."

Frederick looked at me. "What's wrong with him is that he's dying. Look at him. He's circling the drain."

I tried to contain my frustration. Frederick and Brenda turned their attention to establishing an intravenous line. Frederick tried unsuccessfully to place an IV line in each of Nicholas's arms. Next, he tried establishing IV access via the jugular veins of his neck. "No luck. We're going to have to do an intraosseous."

Whereas an IV line goes directly into a vein, intraosseous infusions (IO) access the vascular system through the bone marrow. In the field, they are used when attempts at intravenous access fail. They can be used to deliver medications and fluids. Brenda slid down toward Nicholas's left lower leg to insert one in his tibia bone.

"While you do that, I'll intubate," Frederick said to Brenda. He crouched behind Nicholas's head and tried inserting an endotracheal tube into Nicholas's airway. However, it stimulated a gag reflex, and he began biting down on the tube.

Brenda glanced at the monitor. "His current BP is 72 over 52. It's too low to sedate him for the ET tube."

Frederick sat in the captain's chair, directly behind Nicholas. "I'm going to call the doc."

I refused to give up. "Can you ask him about Narcan?"

My request was met with silence. Frederick dialed medical control and gave his report. "I'm on board with a 68-year-old unresponsive, hypotensive male with a respiratory rate of 6, currently assisting ventilations with a BVM. Attempted intubation but unable due to a gag reflex. Patient cannot be sedated for intubation due to low blood pressure. We just established IO access in the left tibia. Blood pressure is 72 over 52. Our ETA is about eight minutes." Frederick paused to listen to what the doctor was saying. I wished I could hear his words too.

"One more thing. I don't think this is the problem, but I'd like permission to try Narcan just in case," Frederick said to the doctor.

My hopes soared. Although Frederick was doubtful, at least he was willing to give naloxone a try.

Brenda seemed more open to the idea that Nicholas could have overdosed. "Administering Narcan," she said, injecting it into the IO site in his leg.

I continued squeezing the BVM, silently praying the Narcan would work. When naloxone is administered via an IV, it works relatively quickly. Since this was going into bone marrow, I assumed it might take longer to have an effect. "How long will it take before we know if the Narcan is working?" I asked.

Frederick pressed the button to run an ECG strip. "If it was going to work, it would have already worked by now."

"Well, not necessarily," Brenda said. "Since it went into a bone, it may take a little longer."

I clung to Brenda's words—and continued to pray.

Seconds slowly ticked by. I kept praying.

Nicholas began moaning. His eyes popped open. He reached up and yanked the BVM away from his mouth.

Thank You, Jesus. The naloxone worked.

I glanced out the window. We were entering the hospital grounds. I held the BVM over Nicholas's face to provide blow-by oxygen.

Things happened quickly after that. I pulled out a portable oxygen tank and placed a non-rebreather mask on Nicholas as we readied him to enter the ED.

"Go straight to room 15," the triage nurse directed us once we were inside. A full team of nurses, techs, and an ED physician met us there. Mason, Archie, and I lifted Nicholas from our stretcher to the one in the room. When I stepped out of the room, I saw Sue standing in the hallway.

"He's beginning to wake up," I said.

Sue stepped closer. "Thank God I decided to check in on him when I did."

If Sue's visit had been delayed by only a few more minutes, Nicholas in all probability would have expired. And if my work meeting hadn't been canceled, I wouldn't have been on the call.

. . . .

The next day

I ran into Sue in front of the Pine Cove Bakery. "Dad spent the night in the ICU. He became unresponsive again in the ED and required more Narcan. He's doing better now. In fact, he's supposed to transfer to a step-down unit."

Nicholas's guardian angel must have been watching over him, setting in motion a chain of events leading to his resuscitation. I thought back to when Julia had said in our ambulance that she is usually the one who prays for everyone. I recalled how worried she had been about leaving Nicholas. I reflected that she must have been praying for Nicholas as she lay in her bed convalescing at the rehab center. The Lord heard and answered her prayers.

19

The Nosebleed

Send me your light and your faithful care,
let them lead me;
let them bring me to your holy mountain,
to the place where you dwell.

PSALM 43:3

Just as she was getting ready to go to bed, Deborah van der Wal felt something begin oozing from her nose. She grabbed a tissue and wiped the base of her nostrils. With dismay, she discovered bright-red blood on the tissue. She'd had nosebleeds before, so she knew what to do. She grabbed a wad of tissues, held them under her nose with one hand, and pinched the bridge of her nose with the other. "Raymond, could you please get me an ice pack? I have a nosebleed."

Her husband, Raymond, found her sitting on a small settee in their bedroom. "Sure, honey. When did it start?"

"Just a few minutes ago. Maybe too much holiday excitement," Deborah suggested. Their entire family—two sons and a daughter, their children's spouses, and eight grandchildren—had visited for Christmas. It had been a picture-perfect holiday full of love and happiness. But everyone had left yesterday, making the house feel empty.

Raymond passed her a small plastic bag filled with ice cubes. He'd thoughtfully placed a washcloth on one side so her hand wouldn't get cold as she held it over the bridge of her nose. "The heat is blasting too. Maybe the dry air caused it."

Deborah carefully placed the bag of ice on her nose. "Could be."

"If you're okay on your own for a minute, I'll go find the humidifier," Raymond offered.

It took about 15 minutes before the bleeding ceased. Deborah placed a towel over her pillow in case her nose started bleeding again during the night. Soon, she drifted off to sleep.

. . . .

I perused the list of selections at the supermarket deli counter. "Could I please have a half pound of chicken breast?"

The deli worker, a hardworking middle-aged woman, smiled. "Of course." As she began slicing the meat, my first aid pager began beeping.

DISPATCHER: *"Request for first aid at 202 Bergen Street for a 74-year-old female with a nosebleed."*

As the store employee finished slicing my order, I considered the possibilities. Realistically, there was no way I was going to make this EMS call. Although I could skip getting the rest of the items on my grocery list, I still needed to pay. I hoped other volunteers would be available to answer the call.

After receiving my chicken, I headed to the front of the store and got in the shortest checkout line. There was only one person ahead of me, already unloading their groceries. I glanced at my watch. It was nearly noon.

DISPATCHER: *"Second request for first aid at 202 Bergen Street for a 74-year-old female with a nosebleed."*

That meant four or five minutes had passed since the initial request.

Rather than resetting the pager, I left the frequency open so I could listen to what was going on. I hoped a crew arrived at the building soon.

"On the ramp, driver only, awaiting a crew," Archie Harris said to dispatch.

I piled my food on the conveyor belt as quickly as possible, bagged the groceries myself, and hustled out to the parking lot. I tossed my grocery bags into my trunk just as my pager beeped again.

DISPATCHER: "Third request for first aid at 202 Bergen Street for a 74-year-old female with a nosebleed."

Our emergency squad is comprised of all volunteers. Since we live in a small town, we answer from our homes, rather than waiting for calls at the squad building. We have set crews Monday through Thursday nights. The rest of the time, whoever is available responds. Usually, it works out. This morning, however, I found myself wondering where everyone else was.

"I'm going to stand down," Archie told dispatch. "You'll have to call Marina Beach First Aid to answer the call."

I pulled out my cell phone and called the first aid building. Archie picked up after a few rings. "Listen, I can meet you at the scene, but it's going to take me about five minutes to get there. You can cancel the request for Marina Beach."

"You got it. I'll head over there now," Archie replied.

I knew the two of us could handle a nosebleed on our own. I flipped on my blue emergency light and headed toward Bergen Street. Overcast skies kept a chill in the air. I hoped my groceries would keep in the trunk for the next hour.

When I arrived on the scene, Archie was just pulling the first aid jump kit out of the side compartment of the ambulance. He placed it on top of the stretcher, which we rolled up to the front door. We rang the bell before stepping inside.

Officer Vinnie McGovern came to meet us. "Follow me. Deborah van der Wal is in the kitchen with her husband, Raymond. She had a nosebleed last night which stopped on its own after about fifteen minutes. It started again this morning about forty-five minutes ago, and she hasn't been able to get it to stop."

When I entered the kitchen, I saw an older woman seated in a golden oak chair, leaning forward over a matching table. She was pinching her nose and holding a bulky dressing under her nostrils. "I'm sorry to bring you out during the holidays," she told us. "It's so frustrating. I just can't seem to get my nose to stop bleeding."

"That's what we're here for," Archie replied. He knelt next to Deborah to take her blood pressure.

I began writing down her name and address on our patient clipboard. "Do you have any past medical history?" I asked.

"Yes, I have chronic A-fib." A-fib is short for atrial fibrillation, an abnormal heart rhythm marked by a rapid, irregular heart rate. Chronic A-fib is dangerous because it increases stroke risk by fivefold.

"Are you taking blood thinners?" I asked. Normally, people with chronic A-fib are treated with blood thinners to decrease the risk of blood clotting and strokes.

"Yes, I'm taking Coumadin. I also take carvedilol for high blood pressure," she replied. Coumadin is the brand name for warfarin. It makes blood clotting occur at a slower rate. Unfortunately, people who take blood thinners tend to bleed more heavily and easily. This could be why Deborah was having trouble getting her nosebleed to stop.

"We'll take you to the hospital to get checked out," I said. "You may need to get it cauterized." With nose cautery, the doctor uses a chemical swab or an electric current to cauterize the inside of the nose. This seals the blood vessels and builds scar tissue to help prevent more bleeding.

"Yes, I think you're right," Raymond agreed. "This has gone on long enough."

"Your blood pressure is 170 over 92. That's high," Archie said.

Elevated blood pressure could also be contributing to the nosebleed. I was glad Deborah agreed to go to the ED.

"The heart rate is 96 and irregular," Archie added. It made sense that her pulse felt irregular, since Deborah suffered from chronic A-fib.

We set up the stretcher by the front door. "I can walk," Deborah assured us.

I put my arm around her and led her outside to the stretcher. She denied feeling light-headed or dizzy.

"I'll meet you at the hospital," Raymond said. "That way, we'll have a ride home."

Soon, we were on our way to Bakersville Hospital. We chitchatted about the holidays.

"My whole family just left yesterday," Deborah said. "Thank goodness I didn't get the nosebleed when they were here. My three children stayed over with their spouses, and I have eight grandchildren too. It couldn't have been more wonderful. I just wish they lived closer."

I placed another dressing over the one that was under Deborah's nose. "It sounds like you had a great time. Where do they live?"

"One son is in Maine, and he just got married in September. My other son lives in New Hampshire, and my daughter is in Florida. We try to visit them as much as we can." Deborah smiled. "I love seeing our grandchildren. They grow up so fast." She described them and some of their funny antics. Before we knew it, we were pulling up to the hospital.

After we left Deborah with the triage nurse, Archie drove me back to Bergen Street so I could pick up my car. I wanted to get my food in the fridge and freezer before it spoiled.

. . . .

Fifteen hours later

> **DISPATCHER:** "Request for first aid at 202 Bergen Street for a patient who is unresponsive, not breathing."

I sprang out of bed and glanced at the clock. *Three in the morning.* As I threw on a pair of pants and slipped into sneakers, my brain tried to make sense of the fact that the address for this call was the same one

I had been to yesterday. But was the call for Deborah again, or was it for her husband, Raymond?

As I quickly drove to the first aid building, my pager activated again.

DISPATCHER: "Update for request for first aid at 202 Bergen Street: CPR is in progress."

I sprinted from my car to the ambulance and jumped in the back. Meg Potter began driving as soon as I got in. "We're responding to 202 Bergen Street," she radioed dispatch. Ted O'Malley sat in the front seat next to her.

I donned a pair of gloves and grabbed the defibrillator and our portable suction unit. "We were just at this house yesterday around noon for a nosebleed," I told the others. Obviously, something had gone terribly wrong since I'd last spoken to the van der Wals.

When we arrived, Ted grabbed the first aid kit, which included things we would need like oral airways and an oxygen tank. We found Raymond van der Wal standing in the foyer. He pointed wordlessly toward the staircase. He wore an expression of complete shock and disbelief.

We raced up the staircase and into a family room. Deborah lay unresponsive on the floor. Officers Jack Endicott and Brad Sims were performing CPR.

Sergeant Derrick Flint was operating the defibrillator. "So far, there have been no shocks advised," he told us.

Deborah's face was blue. It looked like she may have had an extended downtime (meaning she'd had no pulse for quite a while). I realized with dismay that the odds of resuscitating her appeared slim.

"We didn't get any information yet from the husband," Officer Endicott said.

"The paramedics are five minutes out," Officer Sims added.

Meg and Ted began assisting with the resuscitation efforts. I went downstairs to speak to Raymond. I found him sitting at the kitchen table, head bowed, hands clasped in prayer. He looked up when I entered the room.

"Deborah was having trouble falling asleep," Raymond told me. "She got out of bed at 10:00 p.m. and said she was going to try to sleep in the recliner. At 11:30, I heard her coughing. When I got up just now to check on her, I couldn't wake her up."

I patted his shoulder. "What happened yesterday after we left Deborah at the hospital?"

"The doctor cauterized her nose, and we were home by about five o'clock. We had a bite to eat, watched some television, and went to bed. I just don't understand what happened," Raymond said.

I didn't know what to say. I couldn't imagine what had gone wrong either.

Just then, medics Rose Anderson and William Moore arrived. I excused myself from Raymond and led them upstairs. On the way, I explained what was going on.

William intubated Deborah, smoothly threading an endotracheal tube down her airway. I pulled the mask piece off our bag valve mask, and William attached the rest of it to the ET tube. "Squeeze the bag once every five seconds," he said.

Meanwhile, Rose applied an ECG to Deborah's chest. "Asystole." Asystole is the "flatline" often seen in movies, indicating death. During asystole, the heart is not beating, so no blood is pumping. Asystole is not a shockable rhythm. That means a defibrillator cannot be utilized to shock the heart. If a person is in asystole, it is usually irreversible and fatal.

Meg, Ted, the police officers, and I took turns performing chest compressions and providing ventilations with the BVM. Fortunately, Deborah didn't require suctioning.

I said a quick, silent prayer for a miracle, but even as I said it, deep in my heart I knew that Deborah's time on earth had come to an end. Due to her extended downtime, I suspected it had been too long for her to be successfully revived.

After working on Deborah for about 40 minutes, Rose stood up. "Stop CPR. I'm going to call the doctor for a pronouncement."

A sadness settled over me. Part of me was still in shock that I had been chatting with Deborah just yesterday. I was glad she had enjoyed one last Christmas with her family.

Meg got a blanket from the rig and arranged it over Deborah. I placed a small pillow under her head. We tried to make it look like she was simply sleeping.

I found Raymond downstairs, still seated in the kitchen. William had just broken the sad news to him. "I'm so sorry for your loss," I said.

"Thank you for everything all of you did. I know you tried your best. My brother is coming over. He'll be here in about ten minutes."

I was glad Raymond had family in the area. "I just wish we could have done more."

Raymond dabbed at his eyes with a tissue. "There's one more thing that you can do. Would you mind staying with me until my brother gets here?"

"Of course not." I sat down at the kitchen table with him, glad to be able to provide some modicum of comfort.

Raymond's brother arrived a short time later. We shook hands, and I stepped outside into the fresh air. William was putting his equipment back into the ALS ambulance. "I don't understand. What do you think happened? How can a person die from a nosebleed?" I asked.

William closed a side compartment door on his rig. "It's hard to say. Maybe she threw a big clot in her sleep. It's possible she has some sort of underlying condition she wasn't aware of."

"I wonder if her blood thinner played a role. Whatever happened, it must have been quick. Otherwise, she would have called out to her husband for help," I said.

"Yeah, she went fast," William agreed. "At least she didn't suffer. I don't think we'll ever know for sure what led to her death."

This first aid call stands out in my memory because we never really know when the Lord will call us home. What started as a simple nosebleed turned into much more. I tried to shake off my frustration and sadness. I'd prayed for a miracle—that Deborah would be resuscitated—but it hadn't happened. Then I reminded myself to trust God and His infinite wisdom.

Life itself is a miracle from God. Sometimes, calls such as this one remind me how fragile life can be. Perhaps the miracle was that Deborah could enjoy one last wonderful Christmas holiday before being called home. I was glad Raymond had three children, grandchildren, and other local family members to comfort him.

20

Survival

The LORD God is a sun and shield;
the LORD bestows favor and honor;
no good thing does he withhold
from those whose walk is blameless.

PSALM 84:11

DISPATCHER: "Request for first aid at 817 Horizon Avenue for an 86-year-old female with stomach pains."

I rolled over and looked at my alarm clock. *A quarter to twelve.* I hurriedly pulled on my clothes. Then I headed outside, brushed an inch of snow off my windshield, and drove to the first aid building. A light January snow was falling, making the roads slick. I was glad I'd taken the time to pull on my snow boots.

Jessie Barnes, Buddy Stone, and Jose Sanchez joined me. "I'll drive," Jessie volunteered. I'm not a big fan of driving in inclement weather, so I happily climbed in the back of the ambulance and fastened my seat belt.

Within a few minutes, we arrived at a small ranch house on the other side of town. We trekked along the snow-covered sidewalk and into the home. We found our patient—an elderly woman with snow-white hair—in the rear of the house, curled up on her side in bed. She waved in greeting. "Hi. I'm Sarah Carson, and this is my husband, Eugene. I'm sorry you had to come out in the snow for me. I thought if I went to bed, the stomach pain would go away, but it hasn't. If anything, it's getting worse."

Eugene, an older gentleman wearing a navy robe, sat at the foot of the queen-size bed. "I hope I'm not in the way. What can I do to help?"

"Do you happen to have a list of Sarah's medications?" I asked.

"Sure, follow me," he replied.

While I followed Mr. Carson, Jessie and Buddy began working on checking Sarah's vital signs. Jose went outside to sweep the snow off the sidewalk and prepare the stretcher.

"Please, have a seat," Mr. Carson said, motioning toward a small pine dinette set. He dug into a wicker basket on the kitchen counter and pulled out a folded index card. "Here's a list of everything Sarah's taking. She's healthy, so it's not long. My own list is much longer."

I began jotting down the medications. "I'm sorry to hear that."

"I had kidney cancer a while back. Just recently, the doctor said it spread to my lungs and lymphatic system."

I took a closer look at Mr. Carson. He appeared frail, like a puff of wind would blow him over. I hoped he had the strength to fight the cancer.

We rejoined Mrs. Carson and the rest of my crew just as they were rolling her toward the front door. "Eugene, I want you to stay home," Mrs. Carson said. "Please don't come up with us. I'll be fine, I'm sure. Hopefully, it's nothing."

He nodded. "Okay. If they make you stay overnight, I'll come up in the morning to see you."

The rest of the first aid call was uneventful. After leaving Mrs. Carson at the hospital, I returned to bed and fell fast asleep.

. . . .

Eleven months later

I slammed on my brakes. Christmas packages from a shopping trip with my date, Logan Fitzwilliam, flew off the rear seat and landed with a thump on the car floor.

Logan turned to look at me. "What's wrong?"

I pointed at the road directly ahead of us. "I think that's a bird. It must have been hit by a car."

Logan frowned. "Well, then it's probably dead, don't you think?"

I threw my car into park. "I'm going to find out."

"You're kidding, right?" Logan asked. He hadn't dated me long enough to learn two important things about me:

1. I love ducks and wild birds.

2. Volunteer first aid squad members don't just drive by the scene of an accident. And I'm not referring strictly to motor vehicle accidents involving people. For me, accidents include any mishaps involving dogs, cats, and wildlife too.

"No, I'm serious." I popped my trunk. I keep a towel back there. I figured I could use it to scoop up the bird.

"Hey, what are you going to do with it once you bring it in the car?" Logan asked.

I looked in my rearview mirror before swinging my door open. "I'm going to put it in your lap."

Logan didn't share my love of wild birds. At least, not to the point where he wanted to hold one. "What if it wakes up?"

"Then hold him tight. He'll be wrapped in a towel." No one was going to talk me out of checking on that bird.

I grabbed the towel and squatted in the center of the street next to the bird. Fortunately, at that moment, no other cars were coming. I looked at the bird more closely. It was a robin. I didn't realize we had robins in our area in December.

The robin was completely motionless. Some of his feathers were pointed at odd angles. The prognosis didn't look promising. I knew I needed to get him out of the road before traffic arrived. Instead of taking time to determine if he was dead or alive, I scooped him up with the towel and jogged back to my car.

"Well?" Logan asked.

"I'm not sure yet." I peered at the small piece of feathered fluff.

"He looks dead. He's not moving at all," Logan said.

I pointed to the gentle rise and fall of the bird's chest. "He's alive. I hope he's just stunned and comes around in a minute or two."

Logan scowled. "I hope he doesn't come around in the car."

I pulled to the side of the road and waited five minutes. If the bird were merely stunned, I'd rather have released him there in his home surroundings. As the minutes ticked by, I realized his injuries must be more serious. I decided to take him home.

After dropping off Logan and returning home, I found a large cardboard box and punched air holes in it. Then I lined the bottom with fresh paper towels. I placed the robin inside and stroked him gently. "I'm going to call you Robin." (Okay, I know that's not the most original name for a robin. But for the sake of honesty, I admit that's exactly what I named him.)

I placed the box in a warm, quiet corner of the dining room in my apartment. Robin lay on his side, unable to stand up. His eyes remained closed. He appeared unconscious. *Poor guy must have a severe head injury.*

I called my mother, a fellow bird lover, and she came over to check on him too. Next, I called my local pet store. They'd helped in the past by connecting me with wildlife rehabilitation specialists. If the bird kept going as he was, he'd need a specialist to aid in his recovery.

The pet store gave me the information for someone they'd worked with in the past named Katrina. I left a voicemail explaining the situation and asking her to return my call.

The next morning

I peeked into Robin's box with some trepidation. I worried that, during the night, he may have succumbed to his injuries. I comforted myself that if he was dead, at least he'd died in a comfortable box rather than becoming a meal for scavengers.

Phew. Robin's chest was rising and falling. He was still alive! However, the good news stopped there. He remained unconscious. His eyes were closed, and he continued to lie on his side.

That afternoon, Katrina returned my phone call. "I can definitely take your robin, but not until tomorrow." She gave me care instructions to help get Robin through the rest of the day and night.

I prayed that Robin would somehow recover and be able to fly again one day.

. . . .

Later that evening

Sarah Carson looked at her overflowing kitchen trash container and decided it was time to take out the bag. The sanitation workers would come early tomorrow morning, so she thought it best to drag her large garbage can down to the street tonight. That way, she could sleep in without worrying about getting it out on time the next morning.

She carried the kitchen bag out to her garage and pushed it into the large trash can. She'd invested in a nice one with wheels a few months ago. Her husband, Eugene, had always taken out the trash until he became too weak from his cancer treatment. He'd succumbed to the disease a few months ago, and not a day went by that she didn't miss him.

Sarah pressed the button on her automatic garage-door opener, and the door slowly lifted. Dressed only in a thin nightgown and slippers, she shivered when frigid outdoor air blasted her in the face. She briefly contemplated going back inside to get her winter coat but decided against it. After all, it would only take a minute or two to roll the can down to the curb and walk back. She reasoned that a little bit of fresh air never hurt anyone.

Sarah left the can along the grassy strip of lawn near her mailbox, shivering the entire time. As she made her way back up the asphalt driveway, she skidded on a patch of black ice. Before she could even flail her arms to catch her balance, the back of her head smacked against the unforgiving driveway surface. She slipped into a world of darkness.

．．．．．．．．．．．．．

"What's up, Robin? Do you want to wake up? Maybe have something to eat or drink? You'll be going to a new home tomorrow." Although I spoke to the little bird, he didn't appear to hear me. Daytime had melted into night, but he remained unconscious.

I tucked him into his bedding and then settled into my own bed for the night.

．．．．．．．．．．．．．

Sarah opened her eyes. Everything seemed dark and fuzzy. And cold. Very, very cold. Why, she was so cold she could scarcely move her fingers or toes. She tried to move. *Ouch!* The back of her head felt like she had been hit with a bowling ball. She touched it with her fingers. It felt sticky.

Gradually, she began to remember. She'd taken out the trash. She must have fallen, for she realized she was on her ice-cold driveway. One thing she knew for sure: With the temperature now in the low thirties, if she didn't find help soon, she would surely die.

Sarah began hollering for help, hoping that one of her neighbors would hear her. Then, she turned her thoughts to God. *Please help me.* She knew there was no way she'd be able to stand up on her own. She hadn't been able to stand up from the ground for years. Now, half-frozen and injured, she realized that was not even within the realm of possibility.

Sarah rolled to her side and looked at her house. She doubted she could crawl up the steep driveway. But even if she could, what then? She wouldn't be able to negotiate the steps into her house. And even if she could manage that, how would she ever reach a phone? No, she'd have to crawl to her neighbors' house. With a groan, she heaved herself onto her hands and knees. Ever so slowly, she began to move forward.

The gravel bit into her hands and knees, scraping her fragile skin. After a few minutes, she collapsed down onto her belly. *It's no use.* It felt like she'd been crawling a long time, but she'd only moved about 50 feet.

Once again, she turned to the Lord for strength and courage. Then she pulled herself up and began crawling again. *I can do this. I'm not giving up.* Although the pain in her head was excruciating, she pushed onward. Each time she wanted to stop and give up, she forced her arms and legs to keep moving. Eventually, she reached her neighbors' front porch. Using every shred of strength she possessed, she knocked on the base of the door with her hand.

No answer.

Sarah turned herself so that she could kick the door. Her foot was so cold, she felt like it would shatter with each kick.

No answer.

Sarah eyed the doorbell. Perhaps she could use the wall to drag herself up far enough to be able to reach the button. She strained and struggled until her shaking index finger pushed the button. Then she collapsed back down to the porch as she heard the chimes peal.

One minute passed. Then another. Sarah had to face the devastating realization that her neighbors weren't home.

. . . .

I woke up from a restless sleep. Worried about Robin, I decided to check on him. I lifted the lid to his box and peeked inside. He still lay unconscious, unaware of the world around him.

. . . .

Eugene, if you're watching over me from heaven, now would be a good time to help. I'm in a bad way. I don't want to die on our neighbors' porch. And I'm so cold, terribly cold, right now.

Since Sarah began her journey, the temperature felt like it had dropped several more degrees. Numb with cold, she wasn't sure if she had the strength to go on. One thing Sarah knew, though, was that she couldn't just stay here waiting for death. She would keep moving, keep crawling.

Trying to ignore the pounding in her head, she pulled herself back up onto her hands and knees and slid backward down the porch step. She peered to the left. The Sullivans' house loomed in the distance, separated from her by a seemingly vast expanse of grass. Their front porch light was on. At this point, it was her only hope.

Sarah painstakingly inched her way across the stiff, frozen grass. As she crawled, she prayed for mercy. She thought lovingly of her children and grandchildren. She wanted so much to see them again. She slithered on her belly, focusing on the Sullivans' porch light. It served as a beacon of hope, spurring her onward.

At last, Sarah reached their porch. She hoisted herself up three steps and crawled to their front door. "Help!" she shouted. Or at least, she tried to shout. Her voice sounded feeble even to her own ears. Lifting her arm, she tried her best to bang her fist several times on the base of the door. She wasn't sure what more she could do. She certainly didn't have enough strength to go any farther. In that moment, Sarah faced her mortality. *I want to live.*

The Sullivans' front door swung open.

· · · · · · · · · · · · ·

DISPATCHER: "Request for first aid at 821 Horizon Avenue for an elderly female fall victim with a head injury."

The tones of my pager awoke me from a deep sleep. I hurried to the first aid building and met up with Mason Chapman and Ted O'Malley. Mason called us in service and flipped on the emergency lights, and we were on our way.

A middle-aged woman wearing a thick pink robe, clearly distraught, stood waving her arms at the curb in front of 821 Horizon Avenue. She began speaking as soon as we climbed out of the ambulance. "Please hurry. It's my neighbor, Sarah Carson. She's in awfully bad shape."

What is Sarah doing at her neighbors' house? I recalled taking her to the hospital nearly a year ago when she'd had stomach pains. I'd taken her husband to the hospital twice over the summer. The first time, he'd woken up with shoulder pain and had pointed to a large lump that had formed near his collarbone. I'd worried the lump was an enlarged lymph node. A few months later, Sarah had called 911 when her husband became profoundly weak. Now, it sounded like Sarah was the one with the medical emergency.

"I'm Bridget Sullivan," the neighbor said. "Sarah lives two doors down from us. A few minutes ago, we heard knocking on our front door. Thank goodness we go to bed late. We opened our door, and there was Sarah, half-frozen. She said she fell in front of her house. Somehow, she managed to crawl all the way to ours. My husband and I carried her inside."

Bridget led us up the front walkway and into her home.

Sarah lay wrapped in a giant comforter on Bridget's brown leather sofa in the living room. Her face was pale, her eyes closed. I peeked under the comforter. She was wearing just a thin nightie, which felt damp to the touch. Mason and I removed the nightgown, wrapped her in a special hypothermia blanket, and then replaced the comforter.

Mason placed his fingers by Sarah's wrist to check her pulse. "It's 106 and weak. Her respiratory rate is 28 and shallow. I'm having trouble hearing a blood pressure. There's also dried blood on the back of her head." He placed her on high-flow oxygen.

Sarah opened her eyes. "Thank you." She closed them again.

Paramedics Ty Fleming and Paula Pritchard arrived. Ty started an intravenous line, which provided heated saline solution. Paula placed electrodes on Sarah to obtain a 12-lead ECG. "Her heart rate is irregular, most likely from hypothermia. We'll need to move her very carefully." Paula explained that the hypothermia placed Sarah at risk for cardiac arrhythmias.

We lifted Sarah onto our stretcher, taking care to keep her warmly bundled. Ted had turned the heater on full blast when we arrived, so the back of the ambulance was toasty.

Sarah kept her eyes closed for the trip to the hospital. She remembered falling but was fuzzy on the exact details. "I don't want to die yet."

"You're going to be okay," Paula reassured her. "Your heart rate and rhythm are looking better already. The hospital is going to warm up your core temperature."

As soon as we entered the ED, the team at Bakersville Hospital was ready. I knew Sarah was in good hands. But I also realized the next few hours were critical for her survival.

. . . .

Later that morning

The sun's rays filtered through my curtain, rousing me from sleep. I rolled out of bed and went straight to check on Robin. When I opened the lid of his box, dark eyes stared back at me. However, his gaze seemed vacant, blank, unseeing. He moved his wings slightly but was unable to get into an upright position. Initially, I'd worried he had a concussion. Now, I feared it was a severe brain bleed.

Later, I met Katrina, the wildlife specialist, in the parking lot of the pet store. "If he's been unconscious for two days, he probably has massive head trauma. He's got only a tiny chance for survival," she said.

Katrina's grim words dampened my hope. Nevertheless, I clung to the possibility that Robin would recover.

A week later

I decided to call Katrina for an update. Part of me didn't want to know how Robin was doing. If I didn't speak to Katrina, I could create my own ending. I could pretend the little bird was eating earthworms and flying among tree branches. This phone call might destroy my fantasy. I dreaded hearing the "D-word."

"I'm so glad you called," Katrina said. "The robin woke up the very next day. He's doing great."

A huge smile erupted on my face. "Can he eat? Can he fly?"

"I have a large aviary in my backyard. He's eating and flying on his own in there. It's a miracle. When you handed him to me, I truly didn't think he had a chance," Katrina said.

Later, I ran into Ted on a first aid call. "My neighbor is friends with Bridget Sullivan," he told me. "She said Sarah Carson is being discharged today."

I marveled at God's handiwork. Two amazing survival stories. With divine intervention, both Sarah and Robin beat the odds and made full recoveries.

21

Eyes Wide Open

The LORD opened Balaam's eyes,
and he saw the angel of the LORD
standing in the road with his sword drawn.
So he bowed low and fell facedown.

NUMBERS 22:31

Alec Waters skillfully backed the ambulance into the first aid building. He picked up the radio mic and said, "We're out of service."

"Stand by. I'll be dispatching you for another call," Dispatcher Jerome Franklin said.

> **DISPATCHER:** "Request for first aid at Pine Cove Lake for a juvenile with a fishhook in his eye."

Alec pulled the rig back out onto the front apron. "Can all of you go on this call?"

Darren Williams clicked his seat belt closed again. "I can."

"Sorry, I'm due to volunteer at the library soon," Jillian DeMarco said.

"No worries. We have enough help," Alec replied.

"Bye. Have a nice time," I said as I donned a fresh pair of medical gloves.

Jillian swung open the side door. "Thanks, everyone. Enjoy the rest of the day."

. . . .

Jillian glanced at her wristwatch. She had enough time to stop at the convenience store before going to the library. She crossed the street to where her car was parked in a diagonal parking space. She waved to the departing ambulance with one hand as she pulled the car door open with the other. Humming, she slipped into the driver's seat.

Jillian tried to insert the key into the ignition, but it didn't seem to fit properly. She jiggled it and then tried to turn it again without success.

Perplexed, she glanced at the console. She noticed some trash, including crumpled paper and candy wrappers. *How strange. I don't remember putting that there.*

She jiggled the key some more. If she didn't get the car started soon, she wouldn't have time to go to the store before volunteering at the library.

Jillian inhaled deeply, noting an odd odor. It reminded her of something, but she couldn't quite place it.

Key not working, strange garbage, and an unfamiliar smell. Realization suddenly dawned on Jillian. This wasn't her car! Her sedan— the exact same make, model, and color—was parked directly next to the car she'd accidentally thought was her own. Redness suffused her cheeks. Mortified, she slipped out of the car and looked around. Fortunately, no one had witnessed her error.

Relieved, Jillian rushed into her own car. After looking around in all directions, she backed out and headed toward the convenience store.

. . . .

Alec weaved through traffic as we headed to the lake. "This call sounds painful."

I shivered. "I have an eyeball phobia. When I was in high school, a broken antenna stabbed me in the corner of my eye."

"Ew, that sounds gross. Did you lose vision?" Darren asked.

"No, but my eye filled with blood, and I had to go to the emergency room. I walked around with one eye closed for a week. People kept asking me if I was an owl."

Alec slowed the ambulance to a halt. "I'm going to park here. I think this is as close as I can get."

We trekked along a dirt path to the lake's edge. Officer Vinnie McGovern stepped toward us. "This is Timmy and his father, Mr. Watkins."

"I feel terrible," Mr. Watkins said. "This is all my fault. We were about to pack up and go home, and I said, 'Let's try one more time.' I cast my line and, right away, I got something. The line grew taut, and I started reeling it in. Then suddenly, the line broke. The hook flew back and caught Timmy."

My attention turned to a young, slim boy who looked to be no more than seven or eight years old. He wore a gray-and-orange winter coat and a black knit hat. I studied his face. The fishhook had pierced his eyelid near the lashes. To compound matters, the hook had also caught part of his hat.

Timmy whimpered. "I want to shut my eye, but I can't." The way the hook was entangled, it was virtually impossible for Timmy to close his eye. Rather, it was stuck wide open.

There wasn't much we could do at the scene. It was most certainly a job for a skilled emergency room physician. We helped Timmy onto our stretcher and rolled him carefully to the ambulance, taking care to avoid bumps.

When we got inside the rig, tears began to roll down Timmy's pale cheeks. I pulled a new teddy bear out of our pediatric cabinet. "He sure could use a new friend," I said.

Wordlessly, Timmy tucked the bear under his arm. Using tissues, I wiped away his tears and patted his shoulder.

Mr. Watkins sat on the bench next to his son. "I better call my wife to let her know what's going on." He put his phone on speaker mode so Timmy could hear his mother's voice.

Mrs. Watkins must not have realized she was on speakerphone. I couldn't help but overhear what she said. "Why did you call 911?" she asked her husband. "Why didn't you just put him in the car and take him yourself? Now we're going to get a bill for two thousand dollars."

"Oh, it's okay," I interjected. "We're volunteers. We're free; there's no charge," I explained, trying to ease their concerns. "We're fortunate we've never had to bill for our services. We rely on donations and funding from our town.

"That's amazing. Thank you so much," Mr. Watkins replied. He said goodbye to his wife and took hold of Timmy's hand. "We're almost there, buddy."

We transferred care of Timmy to the nursing staff at the hospital. It was truly a miracle he didn't lose vision in his eye. However, the call didn't do anything to help ease my eyeball phobia.

. . . .

Jillian placed the items she planned to purchase on the convenience store counter.

The clerk, an older man with a silver mustache and beard, calculated the cost. "That'll be eighteen dollars and forty-six cents."

"Okay." Jillian kept her wallet in her purse. She reached for her pocketbook, then realized with a jolt that it wasn't slung over her shoulder like it usually was. *No wallet, no purse, no money.* "I'm so sorry. I'm going to have to come back later." Embarrassed, she quickly backpedaled out of the store. *Where in the world could I have left my purse?*

As Jillian climbed back into her car, it hit her. Her purse was in the front seat of the car. Not *her* car. The other car! The car she'd gotten into by mistake. When she had sat down, she must have placed it onto the passenger seat like she always did. What if the car was gone? And her purse with it? She said a quick, fervent prayer that she would get her purse back.

Jillian raced back toward the first aid building. As she turned the corner, she let out an enormous sigh of relief. The car that looked just like hers was still there, parked in the same place. She could simply pull in, grab her purse, and take off. Hopefully, no one would think she was stealing it.

The parking space she had recently vacated was still open. She pulled in directly next to the identical-looking car. Her elation was short lived. There was a man sitting in the driver's seat.

She tapped on his passenger-side window. He glanced at her and rolled the window down.

"Hey there. Do you mind if I just grab my purse?" Jillian asked.

The man's eyebrows drew together as he eyed her with suspicion. "Pardon me?"

Jillian pointed to the pocketbook on the front seat of his car and gave her best "I'm really a nice person and not some kind of crazy thief" smile.

He didn't buy it. Jillian feared he might call the police. She quickly explained the entire situation to him. With that, she snatched her purse and bolted back to her own car. She recognized it was truly a miracle that the other car was still there and that she managed to get her pocketbook safely back. All she could hope was that the car owner wouldn't decide to check out a book from the library.

22

Too Much Turkey?

I praise you because I am fearfully and wonderfully made;
your works are wonderful,
I know that full well.

PSALM 139:14

Even though it was the day after Thanksgiving, the sun's rays filled our yard with brightness and warmth. With the temperature creeping into the low sixties, it was a perfect day to put up Christmas decorations. Just as I was stringing a garland along our porch railing, my pager began beeping.

DISPATCHER: "Request for first aid at 908 Crestview Drive for a 69-year-old male with difficulty breathing."

When I arrived at the first aid building, Jessie Barnes was pulling the ambulance out onto the front apron. I climbed aboard with Helen McGuire, Buddy Stone, and Jose Sanchez.

"The medics have a ten-minute ETA," Dispatcher Jerome Franklin said.

Jessie flipped on the emergency lights, and we began rolling. "Put us in service."

Within two minutes, we arrived at a brown cedar-shake split-level home. Colorful orange and purple mums lined the walkway to the front porch, where an older woman wearing a floral apron greeted us. "Justin is upstairs. I'm his wife, Anastasia. He can't seem to catch his breath." She led us up a short flight of stairs and down a hallway to a small, dimly lit bedroom.

Sergeant Derrick Flint was in the process of applying high-flow oxygen at 15 liters per minute via a non-rebreather mask. "Mr. Simmons went out last night with his family to a restaurant for Thanksgiving dinner."

Justin sat perched at the edge of his bed. His pasty-white complexion contrasted with his navy plaid pajamas. A fine sheen of perspiration glistened on his face as he struggled to get air into his lungs. He looked up as we entered the room. Due to his shortness of breath, he could only speak in single words and short phrases. "I…ate…too…much…turkey."

Anastasia stepped off to the side to give us more room to work. "Justin began vomiting at about ten o'clock last night. Soon after that, he had diarrhea. I think he has food poisoning."

Just then, Justin began heaving. I slipped off the oxygen mask and held a pink emesis basin in front of him to catch the vomit.

Anastasia passed me a moist washcloth so I could wipe his mouth. "He began having trouble breathing at about two thirty this morning. At that point, he'd vomited so much that I moved him here into the guest room."

It was nearly eleven o'clock in the morning. "Why didn't you call 911 sooner?" Buddy asked.

"Justin thought he had a bad case of indigestion that would pass on its own. Of course, now I wish I hadn't listened to him," Anastasia replied. She opened the curtains to brighten the bedroom.

Jessie slipped a pulse oximeter onto Justin's finger. "I can't get a reading," he said after a moment. "His finger feels cold, so that may be affecting it." He placed his fingers on Justin's wrist. "I can't feel a radial pulse well enough to measure it. It's very weak."

I put the oxygen mask back on Justin and then took his blood pressure. "It's extremely hard to hear, but I got it at 146 over 80. His respiratory rate is 30 and shallow." Justin's breathing rate was well above normal. I placed the stethoscope on his chest, listening to various spots. He was in acute respiratory distress.

While we worked on getting vital signs, Helen pulled Anastasia aside to record Justin's medical history, medications, allergies, and date of birth.

"Let's get him on the stair chair," Jessie said. We'd be able to use the chair to glide Justin down the staircase. We wanted to keep his exertion to an absolute minimum.

Jose and Jessie pivoted Justin from the bed to the stair chair. As soon as Justin sat down, he yanked at the oxygen mask. I could read the panic in his eyes. "I can't breathe," he said.

Just then, paramedics Arthur Williamson and Kennisha Smythe squeezed into the room. "Since you already have him ready to go, we'll set up in the ambulance. He's going to need a breathing treatment," Kennisha said.

"Okay. He has a history of myocardial infarction and COPD," Helen said.

COPD (chronic obstructive pulmonary disease) is characterized by obstructed airflow in the lungs. It includes emphysema and chronic bronchitis. Although it's a chronic condition that tends to worsen over time, people with COPD can have acute exacerbations. But vomiting and diarrhea are not typically part of a COPD flare-up. My guess was that Justin's COPD was interacting with a concurrent medical emergency.

Jessie and Buddy rolled Justin down the hallway in the stair chair. I trailed behind, carrying our first aid bag. As we passed by a different bedroom, I peeked in. Dark-colored vomit stained the walls on one side of the bedroom. I wondered if there was blood mixed in with it.

Jessie and Buddy maneuvered the stair chair down the stairs and outside. We lifted Mr. Simmons directly from the chair onto our stretcher and covered him with a blanket.

I then led Mrs. Simmons to the ambulance and helped her into the front seat.

"I'm really worried about Justin," she told me. "I think this is more than just indigestion from eating too much last night."

I helped her strap her seat belt. "The medics are going to give him something right now to make it easier for him to breathe."

Once we pushed the stretcher into the ambulance, Arthur and Kennisha immediately got to work. Arthur switched Justin from the non-rebreather mask to the breathing treatment. "You can put him on nasal oxygen, as well, at six liters per minute," Arthur told me.

Justin rated his difficulty breathing as an eight out of ten. I turned the oxygen port to six and placed the nasal cannula prongs in his nose. As I looped the tubing around his ears, I noticed he wore a large silver religious medal around his neck.

Kennisha applied a 12-lead ECG to assess Justin's heart rate and rhythm. "Normal sinus rhythm, but he's tachy at 130." Tachy is short for tachycardia, which is a rapid heart rate.

"Can one of you drive our ambulance?" Arthur asked. That would allow both paramedics to continue working on Justin.

"I can," Jose volunteered.

Arthur tossed him the keys. "Thanks."

"I'll stay in town in case there's another call," Helen said.

Jessie slipped back behind the steering wheel. Buddy and Arthur sat on the bench next to Justin; Kennisha took the captain's chair near Justin's head; and I sat in the small side seat on Justin's right side.

Arthur established an intravenous line in Justin's left arm and took blood samples. "Is it getting any easier to breathe?"

"Yes, I feel a little better," Justin replied. I noticed that some of the perspiration on his face had dried up.

"How would you rate your difficulty breathing now?" Arthur asked.

"It's down to a two out of ten." Justin was no longer panting, though he still couldn't speak in full sentences without breaks. Hopefully, he'd turned a corner. I held his shoulder to comfort him.

Unfortunately, the improvement didn't last. Just as we approached the ED, Justin's breathing dramatically deteriorated. "I...can't... breathe."

"We're almost at the hospital. Hang in there," I said.

Arthur passed me the non-rebreather mask. "The breathing treatment is done. You can switch him back to this."

Kennisha called ahead as we entered the hospital grounds. "We need a respiratory therapist and a CPAP machine." CPAP stands for continuous positive airway pressure. It's a machine that pumps a steady flow of air at a constant pressure into the lungs to help keep the airways open. Typically, it's used for conditions like heart failure and obstructive sleep apnea.

When we arrived at Bakersville ED, we took Justin directly to the triage station. "Go straight to room 3," Maggie Summers, the triage nurse, said.

A respiratory therapist with a CPAP was waiting for us in room 3 as requested. We used a draw sheet to move Justin from our stretcher to the hospital's. I gave his hand one last squeeze and slipped out of the room. I prayed the CPAP would help. Regardless, I knew he had a tough road ahead of him.

. . . .

A week later

I ran into Helen at the post office. "You just missed Mrs. Simmons," she told me. "She said Justin is still in the hospital. He was in acute renal failure and started on dialysis the next day. He also has internal bleeding, and they're working on figuring out where it is exactly."

"He was in rough shape," I said. "I hope they find some treatment options for him."

"The good news is that the doctors don't think he'll have to stay on dialysis for long. It's just to get him through this episode," Helen added.

"That's great."

Hopefully, Justin was on the road to recovery. I guess it wasn't "too much turkey" after all.

23

Beating the Odds

*Jesus went throughout Galilee, teaching in their
synagogues, proclaiming the good news of the kingdom,
and healing every disease and sickness among the people.*

MATTHEW 4:23

> **DISPATCHER:** "Request for first aid at 119 Clementine Road for a
> 55-year-old female with chest pain and difficulty breathing.
> This is your second request."

I was just finishing up a daytime shift as a special officer (aka beach cop). I parked my police bike in the garage behind headquarters and jogged next door to the first aid building.

As I pulled the ambulance out onto the front apron, I picked up the mic. "On the ramp awaiting a crew, driver only." I looked to the right and left but didn't see any members coming. If someone didn't arrive soon, we'd have to call a neighboring town for aid. A droplet of perspiration dripped down the back of my neck. I cranked up the air conditioning.

> **DISPATCHER:** "Be advised, you now have one member at the
> scene."

I wondered which of our members had gone straight to Clementine Road. Just then, Buddy Stone slipped into the passenger seat next to me. "Put us in service," I told the dispatcher.

The scene of the call was about a mile away. I flipped on the emergency lights and began rolling. A few minutes later, we pulled up in front of a small white cottage with a screened-in front porch. Bright sunflowers lined the walkway. "We're on location," I radioed dispatch.

Officer Vinnie McGovern stepped out of the cottage and joined us by the ambulance to help carry in equipment. He filled us in as we walked. "Helen McGuire's inside doing the assessment. The patient is Alexandra Owens, age 55. She began experiencing chest pain about three hours ago. She delayed calling 911 because she hoped it would go away, but it's getting worse, so she decided to go to the hospital. She also has difficulty breathing."

My eyes adjusted as I entered the dimly lit cottage. A middle-aged brunette sat in a plaid recliner in the living room. Helen was taking her blood pressure.

Helen removed the blood pressure cuff from Alexandra's right arm. "This is Alexandra. Her blood pressure is 140 over 90 and her pulse is 100, regular and strong. Her respiratory rate is 24, and her pulse ox is 92 percent, so I put her on high-flow oxygen. Her lung sounds are abnormal. She rates her chest pain as ten out of ten and describes it as crushing in nature."

I jotted the information down on our patient clipboard. "How about past medical history?"

"No history, no allergies, no meds," Helen replied.

Alexandra leaned forward in her chair and rested her forearms on her thighs. "I've never felt this awful in my entire life. It came on so suddenly. I just can't seem to get air in, and my chest hurts so bad."

We didn't waste any time moving Alexandra onto our stretcher and out to the ambulance. Helen was on her way to work, so Buddy hopped into the driver's seat, and I climbed into the back with Alexandra. I switched the portable oxygen tank to our larger onboard unit and began rechecking her vital signs just as paramedics Rose Anderson and William Moore arrived. After I gave my report, they began assessing Alexandra.

"William, I can handle this. Let's get moving," Rose suggested. William stepped out to drive their ambulance, while Rose performed a 12-lead ECG and started an IV line.

I thought perhaps that Alexandra was having a heart attack, but Rose said her ECG looked normal. There was no easy explanation for her severe symptoms.

Obviously frightened, Alexandra reached toward me and took hold of my hand. I squeezed hers firmly, holding it until we arrived at the hospital.

Alexandra presented with a complex medical picture. I hoped the ER physician would diagnose her quickly and alleviate her symptoms.

Two weeks later

I ran into Officer McGovern on a first aid call for a young man who had injured his knee playing soccer. "Do you remember the woman from Clementine Road who had the chest pain two weeks ago?" he asked.

I paused from putting our splints back in a side compartment of the ambulance. "I sure do. I've been wondering how she made out. Have you heard anything?"

"They found a large abscess on her lung. She had emergency surgery, and she's been in a coma ever since."

I suppressed a shiver. *Poor Alexandra.* "I wonder what went wrong. Do you know her prognosis?"

Officer McGovern picked up a splint that had slipped out of my hand and passed it to me. "No, I'm afraid not. I'll let you know if I hear anything else."

I wondered why Alexandra had developed a lung abscess in the first place. I hoped she would rally her strength and recover.

. . . .

Four weeks later

Buddy Stone backed the ambulance into our building. We'd just returned from a first aid call for a man who drank a bottle of wine, fell, and cut his head. "I'll mark it up," Ted O'Malley said.

I was in a hurry to get home because I didn't want to miss an episode of one of my favorite television shows. As I looked around for my car, I groaned. I forgot I'd parked it at the scene of the last first aid call.

Colleen Harper smiled. "I've done that before too. I once went on four calls in a row and couldn't remember where my car was. I'll give you a ride in a sec. Just let me restock the cold packs."

DISPATCHER: "Request for first aid at 1403 Sunset Drive for an 81-year-old male in cardiac arrest."

My adrenaline surged. All thoughts of getting my car and watching TV vanished. We jumped back into the ambulance. Since we were all already at the building, we'd be able to get to the scene quickly. That would shave a few minutes off our response time and thus increase the chance of resuscitating our victim.

"We're responding to Sunset Drive," Buddy told dispatch.

I grabbed the defibrillator and suction unit, so I'd be ready to hustle into the house when we arrived.

Buddy parked in front of a large cream-colored Colonial. We sprinted along the front walk and burst through the front doors. An elderly woman stood in the foyer. "Everyone's upstairs," she said, pointing to a large, sweeping staircase.

We rushed upstairs and followed the sound of voices to a second-floor kitchenette toward the rear of the house. Expecting to find our police officers performing CPR, I was pleasantly surprised to find our patient conscious and speaking instead. "I'm not sure what happened," he said. "I started feeling a warm flush go through my body. Then everything went dark."

The woman who had directed us when we first arrived entered the room behind us. "I'm Jane, and this is my husband, Aaron Hunter, and my daughter, Clarissa," she said, gesturing to our patient and another woman. "Aaron was eating supper. Suddenly, he stopped talking and got a faraway look in his eyes. Then he slumped over. We couldn't wake him up."

"That's when I called 911," Clarissa piped in.

Jane put her arm around Clarissa's shoulders. "We lifted Aaron out of his chair and laid him on the floor. The dispatcher told us how to check for a pulse. While we were checking it, he came around."

"I feel fine now," Aaron said. "If you just help me back up, I'm sure I'll be okay."

"Why don't we start off by checking your blood pressure and pulse?" Colleen put the cuff around Aaron's right upper arm and pumped it up. "Blood pressure is 94 over 62, and heart rate is 92. Your blood pressure is low. That may be why you passed out."

"I'm calling your doctor," Jane said and stepped out of the room. She returned a few minutes later. "Dr. Michaels said you should go to the hospital."

I slipped out of the room to get our stair chair. But when I arrived at the bottom of the stairs, I paused in confusion. I didn't see the front door. Nothing looked familiar. In fact, everything seemed different. Instead of being in the foyer, I'd ended up in their family room. When we'd initially arrived on the scene, I'd rushed in because I thought it was a CPR call. I hadn't paid much attention as I'd hurried in and climbed up the staircase.

I turned around. The stairs behind me must be a second staircase. They had a floral runner like the other steps but were perhaps a tad narrower. I didn't want to start wandering around their first floor. I decided to go back to the second floor and try to locate the correct staircase.

When I reached the top, I bumped into Officer McGovern in the hallway. "Let me guess, wrong staircase?"

I nodded. "This place is huge."

"I did the same thing." He pointed to a different set of stairs a little farther down the hallway. "That's the set that takes you to the front of the house."

"Thanks." Things went smoother from there. As I was getting the stair chair out of the rig, paramedics Rose and William arrived.

"Hey, remember the woman from Clementine Road?" Rose asked.

I rolled the stair chair closer to her. "Yes, the one with chest pains who is in a coma?"

Rose slipped the strap of her airway bag over her shoulder. "That's right. Alexandra. She finally woke up yesterday."

I smiled. "That's great news. Thanks so much for the update." After six weeks in a coma, I imagined Alexandra had a tough road ahead of her. "Did they figure out why she got the lung abscess?" I asked as we headed into the house.

"She was diagnosed with granulomatosis with polyangiitis," Rose replied.

At the time, I was still in college. I'd never heard of that disease. It sounded like Rose was speaking a foreign language. "What's that?"

"It's also known as Wegener's disease. It's rare. It inflames the blood vessels and can attack the eyes, ears, nose, throat, lungs, kidneys, skin, and nerves," she replied.

"That sounds horrible. I hope she'll be okay." On the way into the house, I filled Rose and William in about Aaron's condition.

William and Rose assessed Aaron, performed a 12-lead ECG, and established an intravenous line. Soon, we were on our way to Bakersville Hospital. I was glad the call turned out to be less serious than we initially anticipated. My heart went out to Alexandra, finally out of a coma but having to come to terms with a serious medical condition.

· · · · · · · · · · · · · ·

Eight months later

> **DISPATCHER:** "Request for first aid at 119 Clementine Road for a 55-year-old female with generalized weakness who is not feeling well."

Home for spring break, I was catching up on sleep when my pager went off. I immediately recognized Alexandra's address. I wondered how she was coping with her illness.

I met up with Helen and Buddy at the squad building. Soon, we arrived at the cottage. The summer sunflowers that had lined her walk were now gone, replaced by residual snow from an earlier storm.

We found Alexandra sitting in the same plaid recliner that she had been in the first time we met her. "I just don't seem to have the strength to get up," she said.

"How have you been doing since we last saw you?" Buddy asked.

"I remember having chest pain and calling 911 that day, but I don't remember anything after that. My family told me I had lung surgery and was in a coma for six weeks. I got diagnosed with Wegener's disease. Then I had to have another lung surgery, but I'm not exactly sure why. Over the past few months, the disease has affected my kidneys. I also had a mild stroke, which my doctor said could be related to the disease too."

"I'm so sorry you're going through all this," I said as I checked Alexandra's vital signs. Her blood pressure was a bit low, and her heart rate was a tad high.

"I'd like to go to the hospital to get checked out," she said. "I want to make sure my kidneys are still functioning okay."

"I think that's a good idea," Helen agreed. "If you're feeling weak enough to call 911, it's worth getting a checkup."

We assisted Alexandra onto our stretcher and rolled her into the ambulance. The trip to the hospital was uneventful. I prayed the doctors would be able to stabilize her condition so she could enjoy life without worry once more.

. . . .

A few days later

DISPATCHER: "Request for first aid at 1403 Sunset Drive for an 81-year-old male in cardiac arrest."

I tossed down the book I was reading for English class and biked to the first aid building. I recalled the last time we'd had a first aid call for Aaron Hunter. It had gone out as a cardiac arrest, but fortunately he'd suffered a syncopal (fainting) episode instead. I hoped this was the case again.

Jose Sanchez was already pulling out the rig when I arrived. Buddy Stone and Jessie Barnes arrived within a minute. With cardiac arrest calls, every second counts.

DISPATCHER: "Be advised, expedite. CPR is in progress. The patient is on the second floor."

"We're in service," Jose radioed dispatch. Cars in front of us pulled over to the side of the road, and Jose carefully steered around them.

As the ambulance raced toward the scene, I tugged on a pair of gloves and grabbed equipment we might need. When we arrived at Aaron's house, we rushed inside and up the staircase. Once again, he was in the kitchenette—but this time he was lying spread-eagle on the tile floor. Sergeant Derrick Flint was performing chest compressions, and Officer Vinnie McGovern was providing ventilations with a bag valve mask. Aaron's wife, Jane, and daughter, Clarissa, stood a few feet back.

"We shocked once with the defibrillator," Sergeant Flint said.

Jessie took over chest compressions, and Buddy assisted Officer McGovern by keeping Aaron's airway open and securing the seal of the mask on his face. I passed Buddy an oral airway and set up the suction unit in case we'd need it.

"After the last time we saw you, Aaron had open-heart surgery," Jane told us. "He's been going to cardiac rehab and overall doing well. Last night, he was restless and stayed in bed until 11:00 a.m. I made him breakfast, but he said he was too nauseated to eat it. He was sipping a glass of orange juice when his head slumped to the side, and he collapsed. Clarissa called 911."

Paramedics Rose and William entered the room. They intubated Aaron and began administering medications like Adrenalin.

I glanced at my watch. About 20 minutes had passed since the police began CPR. I feared Aaron's chances of resuscitation were slipping away.

Squad members rotate performing chest compressions so that we won't tire. "Andrea, I need you to take over compressions next," Jessie said.

I knelt beside Aaron and placed my clasped hands on his chest.

William looked at the heart monitor. "Before you start, check for a pulse."

I placed my fingers on the side of Aaron's neck. "I have a strong carotid." My heart filled with hope.

William felt for a pulse on Aaron's other carotid artery. "I do too. Hold chest compressions."

I checked Aaron's blood pressure. "It's 140 over 100." I felt for a radial pulse as well. "His pulse is 100, strong and regular."

We rolled Aaron onto a Reeves (collapsible stretcher). Although his heart was beating, he wasn't breathing and remained unresponsive.

Sergeant Flint and Officer McGovern carried him downstairs. Jessie backed them up, and I followed behind holding the heart monitor and oxygen tank. Jose had set up the stretcher right outside the front door.

After we loaded the stretcher into the rig, Jessie turned to me. "It sure would be nice to have a save. We haven't had one in a while."

I nodded my head in agreement. I understand that sometimes it's simply time for people to transition from life on earth to heaven. But as first responders, we want to save *everyone*.

. . . .

We later learned that after a week in intensive care, Aaron was discharged to a rehabilitation center. A few months after that, we found out Alexandra was doing much better too. The doctors adjusted her medications, so she was able to begin enjoying life once more.

24

Orchestrating a Miracle

You are the God who performs miracles;
you display your power among the peoples.

PSALM 77:14

After enjoying an early-morning workout at the gym, Jay Shields slid behind the wheel of his blue Corvette and headed home. He flipped through the radio stations until he found a song he liked and began humming along.

His wife, Kristen, preferred walking on the boardwalk to a tread-mill at the gym. He figured she was most likely out for a walk right now. He glanced out his car window toward the east but couldn't see the boardwalk through the thick dunes.

He turned his attention back to the road, enjoying driving his prized car. The Corvette was his baby, and he loved keeping it in tip-top condition.

· · · · · · · · · · · · ·

Cooper Nolan rolled down his car window, enjoying the cool sea breeze. The salty smell, which reminded him of surfing, never failed to put him in a chipper mood. He wondered if there were any good waves today. He was on his way to work now but planned to be done by 3:00 p.m. That would leave him a few hours to catch some waves.

Cooper noted the Corvette driving directly in front of him. *Nice wheels.* He'd love to have one of his own one day. Right now, however, he was focused on paying off his college debt.

Without warning, the Corvette suddenly veered to the right. It crashed up and over the curb, coming to a halt in the thick dune grass. Smoke began pouring from the underbelly of the vehicle.

Cooper slammed on his brakes, swung open his car door, and began racing toward the Corvette. He half expected the driver to climb out of the car, but no one appeared. *I need to get him out before the car is engulfed in flames.*

Cooper yanked the driver's side door open. An unconscious middle-aged man lay slumped across the steering wheel. Cooper knew the man's life was at stake. Ignoring the danger and risk of injury to himself, he wrapped his arms around the man's torso and pulled him from the vehicle. Cooper dragged him far enough away that if the car suddenly caught on fire, they would be out of the flames' reach.

. . . .

Directly across the street, Pine Cove volunteer emergency medical technician Joshua DeMartin sensed a commotion. He shut off his lawn mower and turned toward the scene of the accident. Yanking off his ear protection, he rushed to help.

Joshua dropped to his knees next to the victim and felt the man's carotid artery. "There's no pulse. I'm starting CPR." He began performing chest compressions.

Simultaneously, a bystander who witnessed the accident called 911. "There's been a car accident near the Shelton Avenue Beach, in the dunes. The car is smoking. I think the driver is unconscious."

. . . .

Two blocks away, Officer Ethan Bonilla was finishing a traffic detail. Dispatcher Jerome Franklin radioed him. "Go to the intersection of Ocean Boulevard and Shelton Avenue for a motor vehicle accident with a car in the dunes. The driver is unconscious, and the vehicle is smoking. I'll be dispatching first aid and the fire department."

"Received. I'll be on location momentarily," Officer Bonilla replied on his portable radio. He jumped into his patrol car and raced to the scene. Once there, he grabbed a defibrillator and oxygen tank from his trunk and rushed to the victim.

. . . .

DISPATCHER: "Request for the fire department and first aid squad at Ocean Boulevard and Shelton Avenue in the beach dunes for a motor vehicle accident. Victim is unconscious. The vehicle is smoking."

Helen McGuire was already at the first aid building doing paperwork, so she hopped into the driver's seat of the ambulance. Ted O'Malley and Chris Nicholson joined her in the rig. Chris, a recent addition to our squad, paid his bills by working as a computer analyst.

DISPATCHER: "Update: CPR is in progress."

"We're responding," Helen radioed dispatch as she proceeded to the accident with lights flashing and sirens blaring.

. . . .

Since the rig called on the ramp so quickly, I knew I wouldn't make it to the first aid building in time to ride with the crew. Instead, I drove straight to the scene. I pulled up just as the ambulance arrived. We carried over our portable suction unit, defibrillator, and rescue supplies. I could see that Joshua was performing chest compressions on a middle-aged male. Officer Bonilla was giving rescue breaths with a bag valve mask hooked up to 100 percent oxygen.

Joshua filled us in on what had transpired. "So far, we've administered one shock with the defibrillator. He needs to be suctioned."

Chris carefully suctioned the patient's airway and then took over squeezing the BVM. Officer Bonilla fished around in the victim's pocket and pulled out his wallet. "His name is Jay Shields. He's got a medical card which says he has a history of mitral valve prolapse." Mitral valve prolapse (MVP) is a condition in which the valve flaps between the left atrium and left ventricle of the heart don't close smoothly or evenly. Instead, they bulge upward into the left atrium. This can lead to what's often called a "leaky heart valve."

"His skin is cool, pale, and dry," Joshua said. "His pupils are unreactive. Respirations and pulse are absent." After another minute of CPR, he rechecked for a pulse. "I've got a strong carotid now."

Since Jay wasn't breathing, Chris continued providing one rescue breath every five seconds. Multiple fire trucks then arrived on the scene. Firefighters began taking steps to ensure the car would not catch on fire.

I went back to the ambulance to get a backboard and straps. A car pulled up and parked behind the ambulance. A group of men got out of the car and stepped toward me. "Hello," one of them said. "I see there's been an accident. I'm a Catholic bishop. Is anyone here in need of prayer?"

"Yes, there sure is. Please follow me," I replied.

As we continued to work on Jay, the bishop, surrounded by an entourage of religious men visiting from Uganda, began praying over him. I realized the bishop was performing the anointing of the sick, and goose bumps swept over me. *Perfect timing for divine intervention.*

· · · · · · · · · · · · ·

Kristen Shields paused during her daily walk along the Pine Cove boardwalk. Through the thick dunes, she could see many emergency response vehicles. It was hard to tell from where she stood, but it looked like someone had been in some sort of car accident. *I hope that's not Jay. I hope his car didn't slip on wet leaves.*

Kristen felt it would be nosy to head down from the boardwalk to the road to see what was going on. In addition, she didn't want to get in the way. Instead, she walked for a little longer and then went home.

· · · · · · · · · · · · ·

"On the count of three, we'll roll him onto the board," Joshua said. As the bishop and his group continued praying, we placed Jay onto a backboard and lifted him onto our stretcher.

Helen grabbed one corner of the stretcher as we began wheeling it toward the ambulance. "How far out are the medics?"

"Six minutes," Officer Bonilla replied.

"Okay, let's not wait here," she said. "We'll get started and meet up with them on the way to the hospital."

Helen resumed her role as driver, and Joshua, Ted, and Chris climbed into the back of the ambulance with Jay to continue his care. I watched as our ambulance pulled away, emergency lights flashing to help clear the way to the hospital.

Sometimes when we are performing CPR on patients, they regain their pulse only to lose it again. I prayed this would not be the case with Jay. His pulse remained strong and steady, which I considered to be a very hopeful sign.

. . . .

Kristen heard a knock on her front door. When she pulled it open, she found her neighbor standing there.

"Listen, I was driving along and noticed Jay's car was in an accident. The first aid squad is taking him to the hospital. I think you'd better go," he said.

Kristen felt the color drain from her face. "I passed all the emergency vehicles while I was walking on the boardwalk, but I couldn't see the car." She began shaking. "I don't even know how to get to the hospital."

"I'm going to lead you there," her neighbor said. "Just follow me."

Kristen felt like she was stepping into a bad dream. But even as she drove to the hospital, she had no idea as to the serious nature of Jay's medical emergency. None, that is, until she was met at the emergency room door by a patient representative, who ushered her into a special "family waiting room." Now, the bad dream was turning into a nightmare. Jay's father had died from a heart attack at the age of 56. The very same age Jay was now.

· · · · · · · · · · · · ·

A few days later

While working as a physical therapist on the cardiac floor, I browsed through my orders. One name popped out at me: Jay Shields. A wave of happiness washed over me. *He's still alive.*

Helen had told me that Jay had become responsive to voices just as Joshua, Ted, and Chris arrived at the hospital ED entrance with him. But we hadn't received any updates since then.

After I reviewed Jay's medical chart, I decided he wasn't quite ready for physical therapy yet. He was scheduled to undergo coronary artery bypass grafting and a heart valve replacement in the upcoming days. Nevertheless, I couldn't resist paying him a visit.

I found him in his hospital room watching television. He looked far different from the last time I'd seen him. Now, his cheeks were a healthy pink. He appeared alert and attentive, like he'd never been sick. A woman with bright eyes and a friendly face sat in a chair next to him.

"Hello, my name is Andrea. I'm going to be your physical therapist, but I also volunteer with the Pine Cove First Aid Squad."

The woman stood up to greet me. "Hi, I'm Jay's wife, Kristen. Were you at his accident?"

"I sure was," I replied. "I'm so glad to see you looking so well," I told Jay.

Jay smiled. "I feel incredibly fortunate to be here. I'll be going under the knife in a few days. Apparently, I have heart blockages, and I need a new valve."

Jay spoke in full, clear sentences. He seemed as though he hadn't suffered any ill effects from the cardiac arrest. "I'm sure you'll do well. I'll be doing your physical therapy evaluation after your surgery."

"We heard that one of your members happened to be across the street when I had my accident," Jay said. "That's absolutely amazing."

I nodded. "Yes. His name is Joshua DeMartin. He's a college student."

"I'll always be grateful to the young man who pulled over and came to Jay's aid," Kristen said. "Some people would have just kept going. It took courage for him to pull Jay out of the car. I think it was smoking because the Corvette is so low to the ground."

"That makes sense," I agreed. "But what really blew me away was that a bishop just happened to be driving by and gave you the sacrament of the anointing of the sick."

Jay's eyes opened wide. "The bishop himself?"

I grinned. "Yes. You must really rank. We've had first aid calls in which priests or ministers have prayed over our patients. But we've never had a bishop. He was with a whole group of religious men from Uganda. They were on their way to a special gathering."

Jay adjusted his nasal cannula. "It's simply incredible. Not to mention that a police officer with a defibrillator just happened to be only two blocks away. I feel truly blessed."

I gave each of them a hug. "Good luck with your surgery. I'll see you for your PT eval soon."

. . . .

Jay underwent double bypass surgery and a mitral valve replacement a few days later and came through with flying colors. He performed wonderfully during his physical therapy evaluation too. God orchestrated Jay's rescue by placing the right people in the right place at the right time. *A true miracle.*

About the Author

Andrea Jo Rodgers has been a volunteer EMT for more than 30 years and has responded to more than 9,000 first aid and fire calls. She holds a clinical doctorate in physical therapy and has worked as a physical therapist in a trauma center for 25 years.

MORE FIRST RESPONDER STORIES FROM HARVEST HOUSE PUBLISHERS

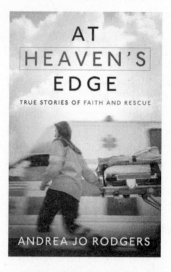

911...What Is Your Emergency?

Veteran EMT Andrea Rodgers has helped hundreds of people in their most vulnerable moments.

Some of the victims faced their mortality head-on and cried out to God for help. Many experienced fleeting but life-changing connections with their first responders. Often these crises became unexpected sources of inspiration.

Now Andrea shares brief, real-life stories of heroic courage in the face of fear. In times of intense suffering, she has repeatedly witnessed signs of God's quiet intervention and healing presence.

- A man is resuscitated after Andrea was able to repair a defibrillator—with her teeth!

- Several bystanders help rescue a young girl who is accidently buried alive in sand.

- Andrea also experienced some lighthearted moments, including the time she arrived at the scene of a crime only to find herself in the middle of a mystery dinner theater.

Experience the miracles and life-and-death drama as you look at life from heaven's edge.

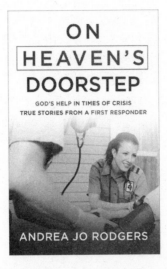

ON
HEAVEN'S
DOORSTEP

GOD'S HELP IN TIMES OF CRISIS
TRUE STORIES FROM A FIRST RESPONDER

ANDREA JO RODGERS

In Life or Death, There's Only One Guarantee— God Will Be There

Medical emergencies are among life's most unexpected and terrifying realities. But isn't it reassuring in times of crisis that you can find hope and comfort in the hands of a loving God?

Encounter heart-stopping drama in these real-life stories of everyday people like you who found themselves on heaven's doorstep—fully dependent on the skilled and courageous efforts of first responders and on the mercy of God.

As you read these firsthand accounts of perilous situations with uncertain outcomes, you will experience a full spectrum of emotions, from tender heartache to tremendous joy. Through it all, you will witness God's amazing love and care for His children, both for those who are brought back from the edge and for those He welcomes into eternal fellowship with Him.

Be inspired as you go on call with veteran EMT Andrea Jo Rodgers and other brave professionals dedicated to helping when humanity is at its most frail.

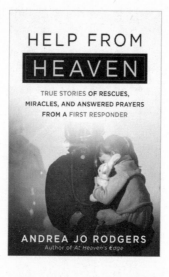

HELP FROM HEAVEN

TRUE STORIES OF RESCUES, MIRACLES, AND ANSWERED PRAYERS FROM A FIRST RESPONDER

ANDREA JO RODGERS
Author of *At Heaven's Edge*

Do You Believe in Miracles?

Experience the heart-pounding drama of real-life emergencies. Veteran EMT and physical therapist Andrea Jo Rodgers shares this all-new collection of accounts from her 30-plus years as a volunteer with her town's local first aid and emergency squad.

Arrive on the scene with Andrea and encounter...

- Lou, a dedicated war veteran who is granted a new tour of duty from God.

- A fearful flock of ducklings that slip down a storm drain during a false fire alarm.

- Everett, a resilient older man who goes for an unexpected ride on the hood of an intoxicated driver's car.

- Jenna, a young woman whose dangerous heart condition is both physical and emotional.

- Frank, a husband whose nasty fall down a flight of stairs earns him instant angel status from his devoted wife.

As you discover these and many more unforgettable stories, you'll be reminded that miracles do happen, whether it be through the heroic efforts of first responders, the Lord's divine intervention, or, often, both.

Quacking Up

In my alarm I said,
"I am cut off from your sight!"
Yet you heard my cry for mercy
when I called to you for help.

PSALM 31:22

When a strange crackling noise slowly penetrated my subconscious, I roused myself from sleep and sat bolt upright in bed. A second later, my first aid pager went off.

> **DISPATCHER:** "Request for fire department and first aid on the 300 block of Meade Street for a working structure fire. Exact location to be determined."

I couldn't believe it. I lived on Meade Street! I yanked open my bedroom curtain. Angry orange flames shot straight up from the second floor of my neighbor's home down the street. The pungent smell of smoke filled my nostrils as it pushed its way through my window screen. I could hear frantic yelling and shouting in the distance.

I raced into my parents' room to wake them up. "Come quick!

The Allens' house is on fire." Without waiting for a response, I rushed downstairs and outside. Although I'm not a firefighter, I raced over to see if I could help. (Side note: As a first aid squad member, I'm a firm believer in running away from burning buildings rather than running toward them. I'd rather let our brave firefighters bring the victims out to us. Of course, this case warranted an exception.)

Fortunately, I found the Allens outside of their home, standing by the side of the road. At the time, one of our neighbors was a paid city firefighter. Like a true hero, he'd already banged on the Allens' door and made sure that they got out safely.

The power of the flames was relentless. I watched in horror as the fire devoured much of the second floor within the span of a mere minute or two. Almost immediately, the fire department and first aid squad arrived. I checked in with our rig and let them know the homeowners were okay.

Our town's volunteer firefighters are top-notch. They quickly extinguished the flames, salvaging the rest of the home. We later learned that the fire had apparently started in a second-floor light fixture. Although the house was severely damaged, no lives were lost. That day reaffirmed my utmost respect and admiration for our firefighters. But it was at a fire call a few weeks later in which they truly endeared themselves to me.

. . . .

DISPATCHER: "Request for fire department and first aid at 349 Shady Grove Lane for a general fire alarm activation."

I hopped into the front passenger seat of the ambulance next to Darren Williams.

"Let's roll. It'll probably be a quick one," he said.

I fastened my seat belt. "Yeah, hopefully it's a false alarm."

Darren turned up the volume on the radio just in time for us to hear Dispatcher Franklin say, "Nothing showing at this time."

"In service." Darren shifted the rig into drive, flipped on the overhead lights, and headed toward Shady Grove Lane.

DISPATCHER: "Update: Owner reports setting off the alarm in error. Roll easy."

As we wound our way closer to the scene, I shifted a bit and suddenly sat bolt upright as something outside the driver's side window caught my attention. "Stop the rig!"

Obviously unsure of why I was yelling, Darren slammed on the brakes. Not wasting a second, I jumped out and raced around the front of the ambulance toward the storm drain next to the curb. I dove toward the drain but was too late. Before I could stop him, the last of five tiny golden ducklings fell between the slats of the grate and down into the drainage pipes. The mother mallard stood anxiously nearby, appearing shocked that her precious babies were no longer next to her.

Darren rolled down his window. "What in the world are you doing?" he called to me from the ambulance, throwing me a look that suggested I might be certifiably insane. Ignoring the question, I knelt next to the drain and tried to pull up the grate. But no matter how hard I tried, I couldn't budge it. It was simply too heavy for me.

I'll briefly digress to note that I love ducks. I mean, I really *love* ducks. It all began when I was in the first grade. While my brother was working on a Boy Scout project at the park, he rescued a mangled baby duck. For me, it was love at first sight. Over the course of several days, my mom nursed it back to health and took it to a wildlife rehabilitation specialist. The experience inspired me to write my very first "book" at the age of seven.

"Didn't you see those baby ducks fall down the drain?" I asked Darren. As I slowly rose to my feet, my mind searched for a solution to the dilemma.

"No, but you need to get back in the rig. We have to go to this call. We can come back afterward," Darren replied.

"It's a false alarm. The ducks need us more," I grumbled. *What if the ducklings are injured? What if they get swept away by the time we get back?* Indecisively, I looked at the despondent mother duck and then back at the storm drain. I could see the five ducklings all huddled together at the bottom.

I shifted my gaze. The fire trucks were just around the bend in the road. It was hard to tell, but it looked like the firefighters were already packing up their equipment. "Great idea—let's get there right away. I can ask the firemen for help."

As soon as Darren pulled up to the scene, I jumped out and ran over to Chief Watson. Briefly, I explained the situation.

"Lead the way. We'll follow you there directly."

Within two minutes, we were back at the storm drain. With a mighty heave, Chief Watson and another firefighter, Paul, successfully removed the heavy metal grid. Paul lay flat on his stomach and reached into the drain. One at a time, he carefully lifted each baby out and counted, "One, two, three, four."

"Uh-oh. There were five," I said. One tiny duckling was missing. *There's no way I'm leaving one behind. We have to find him.*

Standing back up, Paul brushed some dirt off his turnout gear. "We can trace the path of the drainage pipe. It must go under the road."

Much to my relief, we found where the pipe dumped into a small basin area. There, just a few feet from the end of the pipe, was baby duckling number five.

I was filled with joy. Suddenly, I was reminded of the parable of the lost sheep from Luke 15 as Paul reached into the drainpipe and carefully retrieved the last baby. To a chorus of rousing cheers from onlookers and squad members, he carried the little duckling across the street and reunited him with his family.

· · · · · · · · · · · · · ·

The Lord God had formed out of the ground all the wild animals and all the birds in the sky. He brought them to the man to see what he would name them; and whatever the man called each living creature, that was its name.

GENESIS 2:19

In Genesis, we learn that God created all the creatures of the earth and sky. By giving them to man to name, He demonstrated we are responsible for them. To this day, saving the baby ducks ranks as one of my very favorite fire calls in which a group of us worked together as a team to rescue a family.

To learn more about Harvest House books and
to read sample chapters, visit our website:

www.HarvestHousePublishers.com

HARVEST HOUSE PUBLISHERS
EUGENE, OREGON